The Code of the Debater

The Code of the Debater

INTRODUCTION TO POLICY DEBATING

ALFRED C. SNIDER

international debate education association

New York - Amsterdam - Brussels

Published by:
International Debate Education Association
400 West 59th Street
New York, NY 10019

Library of Congress Cataloging-in-Publication Data

Snider, Alfred.
  The code of the debater : introduction to policy debating / Alfred C. Snider.
      p. cm.
  ISBN 978-1-932716-41-2

  1. Debates and debating. I. Title.
  PN4181.S65 2008
  808.53--dc22

                                2008020463

Design by Kathleen Hayes
Printed in the USA

 **IDEBATE Press**

Contents

Acknowledgments

While my name is on the cover and I am very willing to accept any and all blame for errors and faults found in this volume, this is certainly not something that I have done alone. Since 1972 I have been gathering and evaluating debate-training materials for my own use. I have stolen every good teaching technique I have ever encountered.

One main source I have borrowed from is the Emory National Debate Institute (ENDI). Melissa Wade and the Barkley Forum at Emory University have been national leaders in developing training materials for new debaters. Year after year they have refined their materials. The 1999 ENDI policy-training manual was the best single debate training document I have ever seen. My sincere thanks and gratitude to Melissa Wade, Bill Newnam, Joe Bellon, Anne Marie Todd, and all of those at Emory who have worked through the years to produce these materials.

Another major source I have borrowed from has been the World Debate Institute held each summer at the University of Vermont. This program has also emphasized producing training materials for new debaters for over 25 years.

I want to specifically thank the Open Society Institute for its support in this project. Its support for this work in its first incarnation in 1999 as a training text for students and teachers in America's urban debate leagues was an essential part of the origin of this text. The institute's drive to bring debate to communities that really need it has been an inspiration to me.

I want to thank the many novice debaters I have worked with through the years who have taught me what works and what doesn't. I have, of course, not fully learned this lesson, and I am still ready to learn more.

I want to thank Martin Greenwald and Noel Selegzi for providing me with so many exciting debate opportunities. I also want to thank Eleanora von Dehsen for her assistance with this text. I owe a great deal to

Lionel Palardy of the University of Vermont, who kept this text alive between 1999 and 2008.

I also want to thank the Slovenian national debate program, *Za in Proti*, and its director, Bojana Skrt, who hosted me during my 2006 sabbatical from the University of Vermont and allowed me to write in a rich environment. I admire the program's efforts to promote debate and have gained inspiration from its members.

Debate isn't just another game, and it isn't just another educational activity. It is a path of critical advocacy that is life changing and empowering. As my friend from Malaysia, Logan Belavigendran, has said, debate is not just an activity, it is a lifestyle. I invite you to learn the code of the debater and follow the way of reason.

Alfred C. Snider

Burlington, Vermont, USA

March 2008

Introduction

Chapter 1 introduces you to the concepts underlying policy debate. It describes the basic elements of this type of debate—the structure of debate competition, the ideas to be debated, and your role in the debate. After reading this chapter, you should begin to feel at home in this new intellectual space.

What Is Debate?

Debate is about change. We are constantly engaged in a struggle to better our lives, our community, our country, our world, and our future. We should never be satisfied with the status quo—surely something in our lives needs improving.

Debate is the process that determines how change should occur. It attempts to justify altering the way we think and live. Debate occurs on the floor of the U.S. Congress, during school government meetings, and at your dinner table. Some debates are formal, such as when the General Assembly of the United Nations debates whether to sanction Iran for its nuclear program. Others are informal, such as a debate with your parents about when you can begin driving a car. The rules governing debates may differ, but the process is the same—discussion resolves whether a specific change should occur.

Why Debate?

Although engaging in formal debate can take time and effort, millions of students through the years have found that it is worthwhile for many reasons.

- *Debating is fun.* You and your team members will become a community, working for and with each other to win. You will make friends and meet interesting people. You will engage in thrilling contests and you may travel outside of your community.
- *Debating is a sport.* In debating, you compete using your brain and your voice. Unlike some sports, which have physical requirements, you don't have to be fast, tall, or big to succeed in debate. Nor do you have to be book-smart or test-smart to be a good debater. Debate is for everyone. If you think you can learn and are clever, debate is for you. You have a chance to win, but even when you don't, you learn and improve your skills.
- *You control debating.* You determine your strategy and pick your arguments. Instead of being told what to do and what to study, you can create your own learning project and follow ideas and issues that interest you.
- *Debating creates the skills you need for success wherever your life may lead you.* Debating develops the oral communication skills that colleges, graduate schools, and employers are looking for. Studies show that individuals with good oral communication skills are identified as leaders and get promoted faster on the job. John Sexton, the president of New York University, has said that the best preparation for college—and life—is to debate.
- *Debate can give you the power to change your world and yourself.* Your voice can be a powerful instrument for change—in your school, in your community, in your nation, and in the world. But before debating changes the world, it also changes you. It gives you new skills and abilities that you can then use to advocate for the changes you want.
- *Debating is for everyone.* Debating is not just for geeks or nerds. Oprah Winfrey, Ted Turner, Hillary Clinton, Kofi Annan, Nelson Mandela, three current members of the United States Supreme Court (Samuel Alito, Stephen Breyer, and Antonin Scalia), and many others love debate, and you can't say they are nerds. In previous centuries power came from the sword and the gun, but in the 21st century it will come

from the human voice and the human intellect. Debating gives you the skills you need to help change your city, your country, and the world.

Part One

Initiation

This portion of the text outlines the basics of policy debating: the format, the topics, and the kinds of basic arguments that you will meet as you begin debating. After this section you should be ready for a more in-depth exploration of what it means to be a debater.

Policy Debate

Code of the Debater explores a formal competitive type of debate called policy debate, which deals with such issues of public policy as taxation, legalization of marijuana, or the setting aside of lands as wilderness areas. But Code also teaches concepts such as critical thinking, which can enable you to anticipate the adverse consequences of policy actions and the difficulties of implementing a new policy and which you can easily apply to any question of what action to take.

The Policy Debate Experience

You may have participated in other types of competitive debate—Karl Popper debate, parliamentary debate—but you will find that the concepts that come from policy debate are some of the most sophisticated and useful wherever and whenever you debate. Policy debate training is an excellent precursor to debating in other formats, and many of the concepts to which you will be introduced are easily transferable to other types of formal debate. The American policy debate community has developed a very sophisticated and involved body of debate theory and practice, but it has always remained the debate format that is most receptive to new ideas and techniques.

If you are new to policy debating, here are some things you will experience.

1. You will work with a partner. You and your partner form a debate team that either supports the topic (the affirmative) or opposes it (the negative).

2. You will deliver speeches in a format that is unique to policy debate. The speeches are called constructives and rebuttals. During the constructives, you outline your major arguments and engage those of the other team, while during the rebuttals you solidify your team's position and explain why your team should win the debate. Each person on a team presents a constructive and a rebuttal speech.

3. You will learn the rules and techniques of policy debate. Initially these may seem strange or difficult to understand, but once you become familiar with them, you will grasp their relationship to argumentation and decision making in a much broader sense. And as you debate, they will become easier and easier to use.

4. In most cases, you will debate only one resolution, or topic, each academic year. Using one topic gives you sufficient time to prepare the evidence that is vital in policy debate. The resolution determines the debate area, but thousands of issues can arise from the topic, so your individual debates are always changing and the debates remain exciting.

5. Students who want to be challenged can participate in debate tournaments against debaters from other high schools or universities during the school year as well as during the summer at various instructional programs after the topic has been released.

The Debate Tournament

Novice debaters may be nervous and unsure about procedures, so before we go into the details of debate, you need to know how a tournament functions.

A debate tournament is an event in which teams compete to determine who has superior arguments for solving a contemporary problem. When debaters arrive at a tournament, they receive their pairings (lists indicating the teams that will be debating each other), their room assignments, and the name of the judge. Each scheduled debate is called a round. Every round in the tournament has a different pairing, and during the tournament, you will compete on both the affirmative and the negative side of the resolution. After the debaters read the pairing, they immediately proceed to the assigned room so as not to delay the tournament. When both teams and the judge are present, the round begins. If you are unsure about procedures, do not hesitate to ask the judge for help. Eventually, you will become more comfortable debating, and your nervousness will subside.

A tournament usually has several preliminary rounds in which all teams participate. Sometimes, a tournament will stage elimination rounds in which teams with the best record in the preliminary rounds debate each other. Once elimination rounds begin, the team that wins a round advances while the other team is eliminated. A novice can benefit greatly by watching the more experienced debaters in the elimination rounds.

THE RESOLUTION

Teams gather in tournaments to debate a specific topic or *resolution*. The purpose of the resolution is to limit the debate. It is crafted in such a way that there are enough arguments on both sides so that the debate is fair. Here is an example:

> *Resolved*: That Congress should establish an education policy to significantly increase academic achievement in secondary schools in the United States.

The goal of the affirmative is to uphold the resolution based on a position of advocacy called the *case*—the arguments sufficient to support the topic. The goal of the negative team is to refute the resolution and/or the affirmative's case. Both teams debate in a series of constructive and rebuttal speeches. The constructive speeches are used to build the arguments that the affirmative and negative teams hope to win. The rebuttals are used to solidify the position taken by each team and to convey to the judge why he or she should vote for one team over the other.

SPEECH ORDER AND RESPONSIBILITIES

Teams debate the resolution in an order that is carefully structured so that each side has adequate opportunity to present its arguments and address those of its opponent. As you will see from the table below, each speaker has specific responsibilities, and each speech is designed to forward a side in the debate. The words in italics are important stock issues, main arguments necessary to prove a case. I will explain these below.

Teams also have 5–10 minutes total preparation time to use before their speeches. Preparation time limits may be different at different tournaments.

Speaker	Time Limit	Responsibilities
First Affirmative Constructive Speech (1AC)	8 minutes, high school; 9 minutes, college	Establishes the affirmative's advocacy of resolution • There is a problem that could be solved—*significance, harm, advantage* • The status quo isn't going to solve this problem without change—*inherency* • Here is our specific proposal of what ought to be done—*plan* • Our plan will solve the problem/harm—*solvency*
Second Negative Speaker Cross-Examines 1AC	3 minutes	• Politely asks questions to help understand the affirmative's arguments. • Asks questions to set up the negative's arguments

(continues)

Speaker	Time Limit	Responsibilities
First Negative Constructive Speech (1NC)	8 minutes, high school; 9 minutes, college	Attacks affirmative and begins laying out additional issues for the negative • Makes arguments against the specifics of the affirmative case—*case arguments* • Argues that if the plan is adopted bad things will happen—*disadvantages* • Argues that the fundamental assumptions of the affirmative are flawed/incorrect—*critique* • Argues that the plan is not a representation of the topic—*topicality* • Argues that there is an alternative to the plan that would be better—*counterplan*
First Affirmative Speaker Cross-Examines 1NC	3 minutes	Same as previous cross-examination
Second Affirmative Constructive Speech (2AC)	8 minutes, high school; 9 minutes, college	Defends affirmative positions; attacks negative positions. (Last chance to introduce new issues for the affirmative) • Argues that the disadvantages are really reasons to vote affirmative • Argues that the counterplan and/or the critique and the affirmative plan can co-exist—this is called a permutation
First Negative Speaker Cross-Examines 2AC	3 minutes	Same as previous cross-examination

(continues)

(continued)

Speaker	Time Limit	Responsibilities
Second Negative Constructive Speech (2NC)	8 minutes, high school; 9 minutes, college	Attacks affirmative positions; defends negative positions. (Last chance to introduce new issues for the negative) 2NC and 1NR should cover different issues—this is called the division of labor between the speakers
Second Affirmative Speaker Cross-Examines 2NC	3 minutes	Same as previous cross-examination
First Negative Rebuttal (1NR)	4 minutes	Attacks affirmative positions; defends negative positions—once again, the division of labor
First Affirmative Rebuttal (1AR)	4 minutes	Answers all negative issues; defends affirmative positions
Second Negative Rebuttal (2NR)	4 minutes	Selects winning issues and sells them to the judge—weigh the issues by persuading the judge that issues you are winning are more important than issues they may be winning
Second Affirmative Rebuttal (2AR)	4 minutes	Selects winning issues and sells them to the judge—weigh the issues once again

First Affirmative Constructive (1AC)—The 1AC presents the case (a problem exists or some advantage is not being gained) and a plan (the course of action intended to solve the problem or gain the advantage) that are the basis for the debate that follows. This debater has the responsibility to offer proof for the proposition, such that the negative must answer the major elements of the case. This speech is the only one that is written before the debate.

First Negative Constructive (1NC)—This speaker's strategy will vary according to the case that the first affirmative speaker presents. Most 1NC speakers attack the specifics of the affirmative's case. The 1NC might also offer her own independent arguments, such as disadvantages, critiques, topicality arguments, and/or a counterplan. I will describe these later.

Second Affirmative Constructive (2AC)—This speaker answers all the major arguments presented by the 1NC.

Second Negative Constructive (2NC)—This speaker extends the arguments generated by the 1NC and responds to the 2AC. He may also enter new arguments into the round. This debater's goal is to spend time more fully developing the arguments that the negative team thinks will be most helpful in winning the debate.

First Negative Rebuttal (1NR)—The first in a series of rebuttal speeches, this speech covers important issues that 2NC did not address. Usually the 2NC and 1NR engage in a division of labor, in which the 2NC covers some issues and the 1NR others. This allows the two negative speakers, who speak back-to-back, to develop a number of issues in depth.

First Affirmative Rebuttal (1AR)—The first affirmative rebuttal speech addresses the arguments presented by 2NC and 1NR. Because this speech deals with all of the arguments in the debate, it is one of the most difficult in the debate round.

Second Negative Rebuttal (2NR)—This speech explains to the judge why she should vote for the negative rather than the affirmative team. The speaker does not introduce new arguments, but instead emphasizes the arguments from the 2NC and the 1NR that he believes will help the negative win the debate.

Second Affirmative Rebuttal (2AR)—This speech presents the last opportunity for the affirmative to make an impression on the judge. It explains why the affirmative has won the debate, and why the benefits of the plan outweigh the negative's arguments against it.

Cross-Examination—After each of the constructive speeches, the opposing team has three minutes to ask questions in order to clarify arguments, create ground for new arguments, and make a positive impression on the judge. Speakers use information or admissions from cross-examination during later speeches to bolster team positions.

JUDGES

Judges decide the outcome of the debate round, and so debaters address them rather than their fellow debaters. Preliminary rounds usually employ one judge per round; elimination rounds use three or more judges. In addition to deciding who wins the round, the judge ranks and assigns speaker points to each debater. The debaters are ranked, with the first being the best, and given points from 1 to 30, with 30 being the highest score. Judges rarely give below 20 and then only in an extreme circumstance, such as rudeness or offensive behavior. Judges rarely give 30 (a perfect score) but will at times want to recognize a particularly excellent performance. The rank and points a debater receives reflect how well a debater speaks, uses body language, and presents arguments.

Judges decide the debate based on what they are witnessing, not their personal bias and opinions or their knowledge of the topic. Nor do they evaluate the validity of arguments. Instead, they determine which team was most persuasive. Judges like the debaters to decide the outcome and to weigh the arguments in the last speeches. They do not like to intervene in the debate more than necessary. After the round, the judge may, if time allows, give a critique of the debaters' performance and make suggestions for improvement. Debaters often learn the most during this critique, as the judge shares how their presentations were perceived and where they need improvement.

The Affirmative Stock Issues: Upholding the Resolution

The affirmative team presents its case for the resolution. The case should be a fairly complete discussion of why the resolution is needed, how the team's proposal operates, and why it will be beneficial. As lawyers build their case for their side of a legal proceeding, so affirmative team members build their case to uphold a resolution.

In a policy debate each team has an assigned side. It is the obligation of each team to uphold its side of the resolution. The affirmative does this by fulfilling a number of burdens during its first speech, 1AC. The team will identify a problem, propose a plan or solution to it, and show that the results of the plan are desirable. In order to win the debate, the affirmative must address what are called stock issues, foundational arguments necessary to prove the need for change. In a policy debate the stock issues for the affirmative are the following:

- *Significance and Harms.* Significance and harms deal with the importance of the problem. Harms are the results that would occur if the problem were not solved. Significance evaluates the importance of the harms. One thousand people being hurt is more significant than one being hurt. Avoiding future harms can also be thought of as an *"advantage."*
- *Inherency.* Inherency refers to the causes of the problem—the attitudes, conditions, or laws that allow the harm to exist. In order to establish this stock issue, the affirmative needs to identify the way in which the present system (status quo) has failed.
- *Plan.* The affirmative advocates and specifies a course of action for solving the problem it has identified. This plan is not as detailed as a piece of legislation, but within reason it describes who needs to do

what and how to reduce the problem it has identified. The plan becomes the focus of the policy debate.

- *Solvency.* Solvency is the arguments that explain why a plan will cure the harms. If the affirmative's plan does not cure the harms, there is no need to put it into effect. The plan rarely solves the entire problem but, hopefully, reduces the problem in a substantial way.

For the purposes of the debate, debaters assume that the agency identified in the affirmative's plan would enact the proposal. This assumption is called fiat (French, "let it be so"). For example, it avoids reducing debate to a question of *will* Congress pass and put the plan into operation. Fiat is generally derived from the word "should" in the resolution. The debaters are debating whether the plan "should" be enacted rather than whether it "would" be enacted. We do not debate whether it "will" be adopted, but whether it "should" be adopted.

The Negative Stock Issues: Refuting the Resolution or Case

The goal of the negative team is to refute the resolution or demonstrate that the affirmative team has not upheld it. The negative team clashes with the affirmative on the stock issues listed above, and it also presents its own independent arguments as to why the plan should not be adopted. In doing so, the negative may address the following:

- *Case Arguments.* The negative will argue against the specifics of the affirmative case. It might claim that the problem is not serious, that the problem is being solved, and also that the affirmative's plan will not reduce or solve the problem. For example, the negative might refute the affirmative's proposal to deter crime through longer prison sentences by arguing that the problem is not very serious (crime rates in America are decreasing), that current legal frameworks are successful in containing crime, and that the plan does not solve the problem (criminals do not engage in a cost-benefit calculation before committing a crime).

- *Topicality.* Topicality establishes whether the affirmative plan addresses the language of the resolution. For example, if the resolution calls for the U.S. government to enact a program of public health assistance to sub-Saharan Africa, the affirmative should not propose that the United Nations enact such a program, nor should it propose a program of military assistance. The resolution is like the "assignment" for the debate. Just as you would fail a paper that is not on the assigned topic, so the affirmative could lose the debate if it did not debate the resolution. Topicality prevents the affirmative from wandering too far from the resolution in an attempt to surprise the negative.

- *Disadvantages.* The most important argument against a plan addresses the harmful things that would happen if the plan were adopted. For example, the affirmative's proposal for harsher penalties and longer prison sentences for criminals may increase prison overcrowding as well as the harmful effects of prisons as "schools for future crime." Every proposal has unforeseen consequences that must be evaluated. A plan may have an advantage, but that needs to be weighed against its disadvantages.

- *Critiques.* Any proposal is based on a number of interrelated assumptions. If the negative can expose an incorrect assumption, the case that is built on it falls. For example, an affirmative team may propose school reforms because they will improve standardized test scores. The proposal is based on the assumption that standardized tests accurately measure how much students have really learned. A thoughtful indictment of standardized testing might bring down the entire proposal.

- *Counterplan.* The negative can offer a reasonable alternative to the affirmative's plan. Thus, the negative can present a "better idea" and argue that this is the action that should be taken, not the proposed affirmative plan. For example, if the affirmative is proposing harsher penalties and longer prison terms for criminals, the negative might propose community service and job training, arguing that these would be more effective in preventing future crime. The counterplan must be a reasonable substitute for the affirmative plan, not an addition to the affirmative plan. This requirement prevents the negative from proposing counterplans that do not clash directly with the affirmative proposal.

Exercises

1. Have a Public Assembly Debate

Here is a chance for new debaters to begin thinking about a topic and get some public speaking experience as well. I have suggested an issue for you to use, but you also can use one of your own.

This exercise is modeled after the old-fashioned Vermont town meeting. It will give you an opportunity to speak in support of or against an issue. To begin the exercise, your classmates and you appoint one person the chair, whose role is to call on people, and then begin the exercise. If you wish to speak, simply raise your hand, wait to be recognized, come to the front of the room, introduce yourself, and say what you wish. Go on as long as you want within reasonable limits. Everyone should have the opportunity to speak, but if some want to watch without speaking, that's fine. As the exercise continues, feel free to stand up and agree or disagree with something another speaker has said.

> *The Topic*: Schools currently evaluate students' abilities and then put them in classes and learning situations considered "appropriate" for their capabilities. Schools should eliminate this "tracking."

> *The Plan*: Students should be assigned to classes based on their grades in school or on having fulfilled prerequisite courses rather than on tracking.

2. Have a Debate Skirmish

Pick an issue that interests you and your fellow students. You can choose any topic, but I have given you an example.

Topic: High school should be voluntary, as it is in Japan.

Form two two-person teams, one affirmative and one negative. Take 10–15 minutes for the whole group to discuss the issues on both sides of the topic, and write them down. The two teams should listen carefully to the discussion so that they can formulate their ideas. After the discussion, the teams have 5 minutes to develop their strategies and arguments.

Have a very short debate using the following format, with the first speaker on each side delivering the concluding speech:

First Affirmative Speaker	3 minutes
First Negative Speaker	3 minutes
Second Affirmative Speaker	3 minutes
Second Negative Speaker	3 minutes
Questions for both sides from the audience or from team members	10 minutes
Concluding Negative Speech	3 minutes
Concluding Affirmative Speech	3 minutes

After you have held and discussed one debate, you can form other teams and debate a different topic.

YOU ARE NOW A DEBATER! SAY THE DEBATER'S CODE AND MOVE RIGHT ON TO THE NEXT SECTION!

The Code of the Debater

I am a debater.

I attempt to be worthy of this title by striving to observe the code of the debater.

FOR MYSELF

I will research my topic and know what I am talking about.

I will respect the subject matter of my debates.

I will choose persuasion over coercion and violence.

I will learn from victory and especially from defeat.

I will be a generous winner and a gracious loser.

I will remember and respect where I came from, even though I am now a citizen of the world.

I will apply my criticism of others to myself.

I will strive to see myself in others.

I will, in a debate, use the best arguments I can to support the side I am on.

I will, in life, use the best arguments I can to determine which side I am on.

FOR OTHERS

I will respect their rights to freedom of speech and expression, even though we may disagree.

I will respect my partners, opponents, judges, coaches, and tournament officials.

I will be honest about my arguments and evidence and those of others.

I will help those with less experience, because I am both student and teacher.

I will be an advocate in life, siding with those in need and willing to speak truth to power.

BASIC KNOWLEDGE

Part Two introduces you to the basic components of debate, teaches you how they operate, and shows you how you can use them strategically to win the decision.

2

The Affirmative Case

In half of your debates, you will be affirmative and, as such, you will determine the focus of the debate. You present a case that contains a number of conceptual arguments that advocate the adoption of a specific plan of action. While these arguments are essential, it is your plan of action that is the real focus of the debate.

Affirmative Advantages

The affirmative has several advantages in a debate. These advantages include:

- *You pick the ground.* As the affirmative, you choose the problems as well as the type of solution you wish to advocate. If the topic is, for example, that the United States should substantially change its foreign policy toward Mexico, you get to specify the parts of U.S. foreign policy you are not happy with and how you would change them. You might focus on changing immigration policy, or trade policy, or the struggle to keep out illegal drugs entering from Mexico. The ideas are in your control. Even when you are personally opposed to the affirmative side of the topic, you can still control the issues to be discussed by choosing the affirmative case and plan.

- *You set strategies*. While all debating involves strategies, because the affirmative case is planned well before the debate, your strategies can be more subtle and therefore more effective. You can set traps for negative teams by inviting them to make arguments you are prepared to answer; you may hide answers to the arguments you expect within your discussion of other issues; and you can lure them into supporting weak arguments that you can attack.
- *You develop your advocacy*. You can decide what you want to advocate. You can propose changes you personally favor and have your ideas tested in a public forum. When you choose an affirmative case and plan that you believe in, you will do a better job of preparing and debating. This may not always be possible, but when you can use a case you believe in, you should do so.

Selecting an Affirmative Case

Many beginning debaters are given an affirmative case to use. Their coach, teacher, or a more experienced debater might share with them a case that others have prepared so that the novice debater can start debating fairly soon. That's a good way to start, but before long you need to be able to develop your own case. Even if you are given a case, change it, add rhetoric, and make it yours. Arrange the elements in a way that suits you, pick evidence to support the points that you like best, write a personalized introduction and conclusion, and make other changes to reflect your personal style of advocacy.

When selecting your affirmative case, keep the following suggestions in mind.

- *Pick a case that has a strong literature*. You will need good evidence, so choose a case that has a lot of articles and books written about it. Don't worry that some of the evidence may not support your case. Because you initiate this discussion, you will always be ahead of the negative if you really know the literature. Remember, there is nothing better than knowing what you are talking about.

- *Pick a case where the literature is slanted your way.* Don't worry if you find evidence that goes against your case. In fact, evidence against your case can help you predict the negative arguments. Nevertheless, you want the preponderance of evidence to favor you so that you can show that the majority of experts support your position.

- *Pick a case that you personally believe in.* When you pick a case that you believe in, you will do a better job of debating. You will be more interested in learning about it, and so research and preparation will be easier. You are also less likely to contradict yourself during the debate, because the case you are supporting fits with your other beliefs and values.

- *Pick a case that has predictable negative arguments.* Choosing such a case means that you will be able to prepare for a relatively small number of negative arguments. You will have a good idea of what the negative team will say before the debate begins.

- *Pick a case that avoids or turns most popular arguments.* Identify the most popular generic negative arguments and then design your case so that it answers them. Better yet, "turn" these arguments: show that the negative's argument actually becomes a reason to vote for you.

- *Pick a case that is not popular.* Negative teams focus their preparation on the popular cases, so you don't want to use the case that is most common in your region. If your case is unusual, the negative team may be unprepared and forced to debate it for the first time.

Preparing an Affirmative Case

Preparing an affirmative case is all about research and organizing your findings and ideas. Research may be one of the most important skills you will learn in debate. You will need to be able to find and use information and expert opinions to bolster your case as well as defuse negative arguments. Debating is a great training ground for learning how to do targeted research. This is the information age, and being able to mine information is like being able to mine gold. Start learning now so you can find some big nuggets later in life! Here are some pointers:

- *Find the best materials available.* Go to the library and look for all types of literature on your subject, including books, professional journals, government documents, general periodicals, newspapers, and electronic resources. Don't start reading whatever you find or you will never get anywhere. Scan what a library has and see what the best materials might be.

  Do not rely heavily on the Internet. Most debaters will concentrate on this source, so if you use library resources you may be ahead of them. And remember that the quality of Web sites is uneven, so evaluate the Web sources you consult carefully. However, you will want to use the Internet, especially about events that are very current. Consult Chapter 14 to learn more about researching.

- *Scan your research materials.* Once you have found a variety of materials, sort them and review the best items first. "Scan" is the important word here. Don't read a book from cover to cover. You will never finish that way. Instead, look at the chapter headings and find the ones likely to have what you want, and scan those chapters first. When you scan a chapter, read the first and last few paragraphs. If you think the chapter might be useful, then scan it a paragraph at a time, reading the first and last sentences. If they seem useful, then read the entire paragraph. This way you read only the paragraphs that you really need, not hundreds of pages of irrelevant information. Don't forget to look up the keywords about your case in the book's index.

  Follow the same procedure with articles and other publications. Learn to scan vast bodies of literature to find exactly what you need and you will be a winner in the information age.

- *Explore arguments that the negative might use against your case.* Make sure to investigate the evidence and arguments against your case. You cannot understand your case fully until you understand the arguments against it. Use the evidence-processing guidelines found in Chapter 15.

- *Sort your evidence by stock issue.* Use categories such as "inherency" and "solvency" rather than subject or key word. You need to sort evidence based on how you will use it in the debate.
- *Identify weak or missing evidence.* Identify and research such evidence or determine how to develop your case without it.

Constructing Your Affirmative Case—The First Affirmative Speech

The first affirmative speech is the judge's first impression of you, and we know first impressions are very important. Make sure your speech gives the judge a good first impression. This speech, called the first affirmative constructive (1AC), sets the stage for the debate. It is the beginning of a dynamic debating process. You will want to build it not only to introduce your plan and the reasons for it but also to set out the direction of the debate. You can design it to anticipate negative attacks and thus make your team's job easier.

Here are some basic guidelines for composing the first affirmative speech.

- *Begin with your thesis statement.* Begin your speech by reading the resolution and then giving two or three sentences that explain your thesis. Make sure that the judge understands your general ideas before you start presenting evidence and subpoints.
- *Keep your contentions few and clear.* Match your contentions, the major points of your case, to the stock issues whenever possible. Word your contentions simply and clearly so that the judge can write them down easily. Don't present too many subpoints; make your ideas sound big, not fragmented and trivial. Don't be afraid to reiterate the titles of important contentions so that the judge will be sure to understand them.

- *Present your arguments in a logical order.* Organize your arguments in meaningful groups. For example, put all the arguments about why the plan solves the problem in one contention. Also, follow a problem-solution format in building your speech: problem (significance and impact), cause (inherency), solution (plan), workability (solvency). This format is easiest for the judge to understand.
- *Remember to include inherency.* You must show that a problem exists and that the status quo allows the harm to continue. A problem can exist for several reasons:
  - *attitudinal inherency*—People, policy makers, or others do not want the problem solved.
  - *structural inherency*—Laws, regulations, or physical constraints prevent solving the problem.
  - *harms inherency*—The current way we are dealing with the problem is a bad one, creating harms. The affirmative plan would solve the problem without these harms.
  - *existential inherency*—Not a very strong inherency. Don't use it. Just be aware that some weaker debaters will. The argument is that if the problem persists, then there must be an inherency that "exists" somewhere out there. Of course, saying that it exists somewhere does not fulfill your obligation to show inherency.
- *Clearly articulate significance and impact.* Explain significance and impact clearly to make the need for your plan seem important. You can do this in a number of ways:
  - *advantage vs. harm*—Advantages and harms say the same thing in a little different way. An advantage says that if we adopt the plan, things will be better, while harm states that bad things are happening now and we need to stop them. Advantages are best when your impact is in the future; harms are better when your impact is in the present.
  - *quantitative dimensions*—The implications of some impacts are clear and need only be counted. We all accept that certain impacts—death, illness, or children in poverty, for example—are bad,

so all you have to do is specify a number in your case. Find big harms and then find big numbers to represent them.

- *qualitative dimensions*—Some impacts can't be counted. You can't assign a dollar value to freedom or a weight to beauty, because these are qualitative concepts. Nevertheless, they are very important. Very few people would sell themselves into slavery, for example, at any price.
- *emotionally loaded*—Find harms that pull at people's heart strings. Show compassion and concern for those you identify as being harmed, because they are the ones for whom you are advocating.

- *Present a well thought-out, carefully written plan.* Your plan is what you are advocating, and is the most strategic portion of the affirmative case. Your plan serves as an outline of what you are proposing. It should include the following:
  - *agent: singular or incentive oriented*—You need some agent to carry out your plan. Certainly you need to use the agent identified in the resolution (such as the federal government), but beyond that you should indicate what part of that agent would implement the plan, for example, the State Department. You also might want to have the agent in the resolution give incentives to other groups or levels of government to carry out the plan.
  - *action: what, how much, how long, model, advocate*—You need to specify the action in your plan. What is it that will be done? How long will it take to implement the plan? You might consider using a model program as a guide for your plan ("We will do nationally what they do in Wisconsin"). This approach makes defending your plan easier since, for example, it already works in Wisconsin. You might also want to identify an advocate, probably someone you have good solvency evidence from, by saying, "We will adopt the school voucher proposal presented by Dr. Ivan Feelgood of the University of Montana." Referencing an expert makes proving solvency easier.

- *funding: normal vs. targeted*—You need to pay for the plan. You can do that by either using "normal means" (money Congress appropriates and the executive branch spends) or you can have targeted funding (such as cuts in an expensive bomber program for the military). Either way, you need to be able to say how you pay.
- *enforcement: normal vs. targeted*—You need to make sure the plan has the force of law, or else people who don't like it will simply ignore it. You can utilize normal means for enforcement (executive branch, using the police and the courts) or you can have a specific agent to enforce it (Inspector General of the United States).
- *interpretation*—The plan you present in your speech can never be complete, because your speech is limited in length. You might indicate in your plan that affirmative speeches will clarify plan particulars if necessary. After all, you don't want the negative clarifying what the plan does.

Remember, when writing your plan, use wording from the resolution wherever you can, because your plan will sound more topical.

- *Be comprehensive in discussing solvency.* Solvency is the most important stock issue the affirmative must prove in the first constructive speech. The affirmative gets no credit for pointing out a problem, only for solving it. Include the following in your discussion:
  - *explanation of how your plan will work and why*—Make sure your rhetoric and solvency evidence explain how and why your plan solves the problem or results in an improvement. These explanations will help you defend against negative attacks. Judges hate to vote for a plan when they don't understand how it works.
  - *range of solvency*—Indicate how much of the problem you will be able to solve. Don't worry that you can't completely solve the problem; your plan will still be a good idea even if it isn't perfect. However, you must be able to indicate a range of solvency: we solve some important part of the problem; we solve half the problem; we solve almost the entire problem. As long as you can solve

some of the problem, you have met the solvency burden, but the more of the problem you solve, the stronger your case.

- *model or example*—Feel free to copy a successful plan. Then read the results of that specific program as your solvency evidence.
- *solvency advocate*—You should identify a specific author who says your plan is a good idea. This may not be essential, but judges generally like you to do so and many negatives will demand it. The judge often likes to know that there is some subject area expert who actually advocates your proposal.
- *overcome the inherencies*—If you identify inherent barriers, make sure your plan can overcome them.

Remember, solvency is also the stock issue the negative is most likely to attack.

Once you have the basics down, you might want to consider the following in composing the 1AC:

- *Frontload needed evidence for 2AC.* Include evidence that the 2AC can later use without having to waste time reading it. For example, you can hide evidence to turn the disadvantages, evidence to permute the counterplan, and independent solvency evidence. Often a good place to hide such evidence is near the end of the 1AC because the negative, which will be focused on developing the 1NC, may not have time to address it.
- *Prepare different versions of your speech for different judges.* Some judges like a slower speech, others a faster. Have two different versions so that you don't have to do last minute editing to accommodate the judge and stay within your allotted time.
- *Remember the importance of rhetoric.* Evidence is important, but remember that this is *your* case and that ultimately you are the advocate. Use colorful but sophisticated language of your own to explain your ideas. Don't just present evidence after evidence; also put in strong rhetorical statements explaining what the evidence proves and why your

arguments are important. Use your own language to explain your case to the judge.

Briefing/Frontlines—Preparation Before the Debate

A brief is an outline of an argument, including claims, supportive reasoning, and evidence. You will need to write specific briefs to answer expected negative arguments. These are called frontlines, your first line of response to negative attack. You predict all of the negative arguments you can and prepare responses to them. As the season progresses and you hear new arguments, you develop additional frontlines. In this way you can save your preparation time for your rebuttals, instead of for the second constructive speech, since you have already prepared answers to much that the negative may charge. Other prepared arguments to be used after the frontlines will consist of other briefs you have produced.

Here are some suggestions for preparing frontlines. Keep these in mind as you prepare answers to anticipated negative arguments.

- *List negative case arguments.* You might want to brainstorm to create a list of potential negative arguments. After you begin debating competitively, you can add arguments you've encountered to your list. You can also exchange lists with other debaters.
- *Create briefs to answer arguments, not just as evidence categories.* Policy debaters use block quotations like one would find in a research paper to prove their arguments. These are evidenced arguments. At other times they use their own logic and reasoning to prove their arguments. These are analytical arguments. Often new debaters will prepare frontlines composed only of evidence. The best frontlines use a combination of analytical and evidenced arguments.
- *Put your best evidence first.* That way you will be sure to use it.
- *Prepare reasons why your plan meets the test of topicality.* Define each word in the resolution and then develop an explanation of how the affirmative plan meets that definition.

- *Draft answers to various counterplans.* Explain why they do not compete with your plan ("it is not an alternative to the affirmative plan"), as well as "turning" the counterplan ("the counterplan makes the problem worse") along with other answers you might have.
- *Avoid contradictions.* As you prepare your frontlines, watch out for contradictions. It is better to anticipate and avoid contradictions before the debate than to have the negative team point them out during the debate.
- *Create an index of your frontlines.* Consider an expando/accordion file for your affirmative frontlines. You can create a list of all of your frontlines, put them in separate categories in your accordion file, and then tape the index to the front of the file for easy reference.

Here are some other tips that you will find useful:
- When answering a disadvantage (where the negative claims that your proposal will cause additional problems), make sure you use a full range of responses, such as claiming no link ("we do not cause that problem"), no impact ("if that happened it would not be so bad"), non-unique ("that will happen with or without the plan"), and turns ("no, we actually solve this problem with our plan").
- When answering a critique (where the negative claims that your case involves assumptions that are false, evil, or both), make sure that you have a full range of responses, such as no link ("we do not make that assumption"), no impact ("that assumption is not false or evil"), and turns ("the negative is actually the one making assumptions that are false, evil, or both"), as well as how your plan solves the critique.
- You may need additional background information to defend your case, such as how the data were gathered, the specifics about your precise proposal, the qualifications of your major authors, and other information.

Exercises

1. Compare sample plans. Write several different versions of your plan and share them with your partner or other debaters. Ask them which is best and develop a final plan from that version.

2. Give a practice 2AC. Identify a number of arguments that the 1NC could make against your case and then give a 2AC answering them. Have your partner listen and make suggestions. Monitor the way you allocate time. As you use your frontlines, adjust and edit them.

3. Practice answering specific arguments. Identify specific arguments that you want to address and then give yourself a specific amount of time to answer them. Work on answering arguments quickly and efficiently as you do this. Repeat until you know how you will answer these arguments.

4. Develop new advantages. Develop some new advantages that you do not have time for in your 1AC, and then prepare them for insertion as substitute advantages into the 1AC or for delivery in 2AC. You would use these at the end of a 2AC if and when you have any time remaining. Practice presenting these arguments so that they are clear and quick. Remember that sometimes you can use these new advantages to turn disadvantages that the negative might offer.

3

The Negative Attacks the Affirmative Case

One of the defining characteristics of debate is clash. Specific disagreement is what judges look for in deciding who did the better job of debating. The center of that clash is the negative team's analysis and refutation of the first affirmative speech—the affirmative case. This section explains some techniques for attacking the affirmative.

General Considerations

You can use a wide variety of techniques in attacking the affirmative case, and it is essential that you make these choices strategically instead of randomly. You need to keep your goals in mind while providing criticism of the case.

- *Attack the affirmative team's claims of harm and eliminate or minimize its impact scenarios.* You must not allow affirmative scenarios to be sustained in the debate. Your goal is to completely eliminate them, but since this is rarely possible in a good debate, you must challenge and limit them.

- *Use case turns.* Capture what the other team is saying and use it against them. For example, if the affirmative shows that it is solving the problem the disadvantage discusses, you can turn the link to the harm ("Your plan makes the problem worse").

- *Knock out a stock issue.* Since the affirmative must win all stock issues (significance, inherency, solvency), you can win by showing that the affirmative has not proved one. Concentrate your attack on the weakest of these necessary components. If one link in this argumentative chain is broken, you may have a reasonable claim that the affirmative case cannot stand.

- *Bog the opposition down—focus your opponent on one issue.* Time during a speech can be thought of as temporal capital, and you need to use it wisely. Often your attacks on the affirmative case can take far longer for the affirmative to answer than for you to make. Time spent on defending one aspect of the affirmative case means time the affirmative cannot spend on addressing other issues you have introduced.

Organizational Guidelines for Attacking the Case

Sound organization enhances any debate presentation, but being organized is especially important for the negative team because it must apply its arguments to the structure of the affirmative case. Remember the following organizational points when attacking the case:

- *Focus on the affirmative's most important points and attack them in the order they were presented.* A strategically wise affirmative team may put one of the most crucial issues at the end of the first affirmative speech and wait for the negative team to neglect it before using it against the negative. Always look at all of the points in the affirmative case, decide what is important, and then allocate time and arguments on that basis. Deal with them in the order presented so the judge can follow them easily.

- *Number your arguments on each major case section.* In a perfect world with unlimited speech time, the negative would analyze each argument in the affirmative's case, but because of time constraints this is impossible. Instead the negative must identify an important component of the affirmative case and launch a number of attacks against it. To save time and ensure that the judge understands which component you are addressing, identify the component of the affirmative case (let us say, contention 1, subpoint B) and launch a number of arguments against that component (which may have several pieces of evidence as well as B-1 and B-2 subpoints). Number your arguments consecutively. For example, a negative speaker might say, "Please turn to affirmative's 1-B subpoint, 'Unemployment has harmful consequences,' where we will argue . . . 1. ARG; 2. ARG; 3. ARG."

- *Centralize your argumentation.* Present all of your arguments about a certain issue ("Unemployment does not cause health harms") at one time.
- *Don't repeat arguments.* Repeating an argument fills speech time but does not act as an effective attack, and the affirmative can respond to the argument easily by answering it once (very thoroughly) and then referring all repetitions back to that answer.

Specific Techniques for Attacking the Affirmative Case

Often the negative has to quickly compose the arguments it will use to attack the case, so you should be familiar with the various forms you can use. These techniques should become "habits of mind" for negative speakers attacking the affirmative case. Mix them up when you attack the case, avoiding too much reliance on one form.

UTILIZING CHALLENGES

A challenge is an argument that indicates inadequacies in the arguments of the opponent and urges their rejection or degradation. It specifically identifies logical and developmental inadequacies in argumentation and then reevaluates the argument based on these inadequacies. The affirmative's failure to address these inadequacies means that the negative reevaluation of the argument stands.

Use a simple two-part format for your challenge:

1. *Specify the lacking element(s).* Something is missing or imperfect about an argument. Perhaps an argument is missing a logical step, involves an argumentative fallacy, or confuses the specific with the general. Point out these elements.
2. *Demonstrate its importance.* Reevaluate the affirmative's argument. Characterize an element in the argument as weak or irrelevant and explain why the inadequacy you have pointed out means that the affirmative's entire argument is logically inadequate. If the affirmative has argued that U.S. foreign assistance tends to help only those already well off, and it tries to prove this by pointing to one program in one country that fits this model, that would be inadequate to prove the larger argument because it is only one program out of many such programs. Thus, the affirmative failed to prove the general statement and it must be rejected. The important points here are that you need to remember how to reevaluate an argument based on the challenge and the use of a challenge not responded to by the affirmative in a later speech.

INDICTING AFFIRMATIVE EVIDENCE

Evidence is the support on which many arguments rest. Undermining this support by addressing major inadequacies in evidence is essential if you are to win the debate. Here are some simple techniques to keep in mind to indict the evidence:

- *Match the evidence with the claim.* Often the affirmative uses evidence to support a claim that is much broader than the evidence warrants. Listen carefully to the actual words of affirmative evidence and then launch challenges against important evidence that seems particularly vulnerable or important.
- *Analyze the strength of evidence.* Probability is a continuum that begins at "absolutely will not happen" and runs to "absolutely will happen." Few ideas exist at either end of the spectrum; most fall somewhere in the middle range. Identify qualifiers contained in the evidence and use them in your challenge.

- *Note recency and relevance.* All else being equal, recent evidence is better than older evidence. However, recency is more important in some situations than in others. Recency may not be an important factor in evaluating evidence about the yearning humans have to be loved, but it is important when debating a nation's intention to acquire nuclear weapons, especially if the situation is extremely fluid. Point out and criticize lack of recency only if events are likely to have changed since the evidence first appeared.
- *Evaluate source qualification.* Make sure the evidence is written by subject experts. Demand source qualifications from the affirmative while making sure that your sources are qualified. Ask the judge to opt for qualified negative evidence over unqualified affirmative evidence in any instance where sources are in conflict.
- *Check for source bias.* Authors are often fervent believers in a specific approach to the controversy, and some sources have direct vested interests in making certain statements. Not everyone who has an opinion is a biased source, and some source bias is rarely grounds for rejecting the evidence entirely, but serious source bias should be pointed out and the strength of that evidence reduced.
- *Analyze source conclusion.* Many scholarly sources evaluate controversies thoroughly, dealing with relevant issues on both sides. Often the affirmative uses only those aspects of the source that support its claim. Point this out to reduce the validity of its claims.

STRATEGIC WILLINGNESS TO CONCEDE PORTIONS OF CASE

Refuting and attacking the affirmative case should be guided by strategy, not just the reflex action of disagreeing with everything the affirmative says. Therefore, you may wish to concede various portions of an affirmative case if that concession promotes your strategic interests. For example, if an affirmative notes that "unemployment causes stress" and that "stress can lead to harmful health effects," you might agree that stress can have harmful effects, but argue that work is a much more significant source of stress than lack of work. If you can use affirmative positions as a foundation for your arguments, your foundation is likely to be strong because the affirmative team has taken a position that they cannot withdraw.

Often affirmatives claim end-states or actions as being "good" and thus advocate these ideas. You can use these end-states or actions as "links," causal or correlative relationships with another argument that you will then launch. For example, when the affirmative claims that unemployment is harmful, the negative might use this as a "link" to its argument that employment is more harmful because of work-related stress.

If you concede a position, don't argue against it. For example, in the case of conceding the affirmative arguments about unemployment above, you should not also make arguments that eliminate the hoped-for link to its other arguments. You should not make statements, such as, "There really isn't any unemployment," against this conceded position, because it may serve to eliminate the link you hope to gain with the concession. If you are going to use one of the affirmative's arguments to build a new argument of your own, do not attack it.

Techniques for Dealing with Stock Issues

Stock issues are those that the affirmative must win in order to win the debate. The affirmative team must show there is a problem (harms, significance); it has to show inherency (why the status quo is not dealing with this issue); it has to present a plan (its solution to the situation); and it has to show that its plan will, to some extent, deal successfully with the problem. Thus, if you can defeat one of these areas, you have defeated the case.

CLASHING WITH AFFIRMATIVE INHERENCY

Do not attack inherency. You probably cannot prove that the status quo is perfect, and you would have to do so in order to win the debate based on inherency. Instead, utilize the affirmative's inherency arguments to build arguments you can use in other parts of the debate. Here are some examples:

- Inherency often indicates barriers that exist. Make the affirmative team prove that it can overcome those barriers, or else it will have no solvency.
- Inherency often establishes that people don't like or don't want the plan. If this is true, then people will try to sabotage it or stop it from working, or it will anger people and lead to a backlash, presenting you with issues of solvency or disadvantage that you can use to your benefit.
- Affirmative teams never give all the reasons why the plan hasn't been adopted or the problem hasn't been solved. Think of what those "unmentioned" inherencies are and use those to attack solvency or create disadvantages.

CLASHING WITH AFFIRMATIVE IMPACT CLAIMS

The affirmative must show that there is a reason to act, that the status quo allows some harm to continue or fails to achieve some advantage, and that either of these is truly significant. Without meeting this burden, there is no reason to adopt the plan. Here are some simple strategies you can use in evaluating and analyzing impact claims.

- *Require and analyze the specifications of a scenario.* A scenario is a specification of a series of events that results in an outcome. Specification is critical: a scenario would not just say that "a war will start" but that "a war between X and Y will start if A happens, and that war will result in B." In traditional argumentation parlance, this is known as demonstration. A general claim ("Unprotected nuclear weapons will be misused") needs to be demonstrated through a scenario ("Unprotected nuclear weapons will be obtained and used in anger during coming ethnic conflicts in Russia, causing millions of deaths"). You should require specification and demonstration of a scenario from the affirmative when it makes impact claims. You can then examine lines of causation and influence more directly as well as expose weak concepts that underlie the general one.

- *Identify mutually exclusive or mutually influencing scenarios.* Examine scenarios closely to see if they can be combined or must be considered separately. Don't let the affirmative wrongly combine events and then claim the impact of their combined importance.
- *Attack impact scenarios.* The affirmative attempts to show that its advocacy is important by providing impact scenarios—if the status quo continues, bad things will happen. This is an essential part of its overall case. If there is no strong reason to adopt the plan, then the negative should win the debate.
  - *Attack value or qualitative claims.* Qualitative claims are usually not readily susceptible to numerical evaluation. Freedoms, equality, and justice are important concepts, but they can rarely be evaluated in numerical terms. But these claims do have a numerical dimension, which is the beginning of our list of techniques.
    - *Challenge the number of people impacted.* Indicate that this qualitative impact occurs in a small number of cases. When one individual's freedom is compromised, it is unfortunate but it would be far worse if millions had their freedom compromised.
    - *Dispute the amount that the value is infringed.* Do not let the affirmative claim the whole value when it is only partially compromised. For example, the affirmative may claim that refusing to allow some high school students to write what they want in their school newspaper is a violation of the freedom of expression. As the affirmative describes its position, it will usually talk about how important freedom of expression is and how it must be preserved. The negative team must make sure that the discussion of this incident does not escalate to an affirmative claim that the entire weight of freedom of expression should be given to this argument, since it is really only a few high school students who have lost their freedom of the press rights in the forum of the high school newspaper.

- *Show that this is not a preferred value.* Indicate that those who are experiencing qualitative losses do not consider the loss serious.
- *Show that this value trades off with other values.* Indicate that by affirming one value another is compromised. Liberty and security, privacy and community, equality and justice—these are just a few of the values that can be mutually eroding in some situations.
- *Show that this value is culturally biased.* Indicate that affirmative values are not very important because they are too culturally embedded. While your charge might not take out the affirmative impact claim by itself, it may make it easier for you to outweigh it with broader value impact claims.

- *Attack factual or quantitative claims.* Here are some common, simple ideas you can use in refuting quantitative impact claims.
    - *Dispute numbers.* Obviously, an event that costs 10,000 lives is more significant than an event that costs 1,000 lives. Make the affirmative prove a number with evidence and then try to reduce that number.
    - *Evaluate the harm of each instance.* Evaluate each instance of the affirmative's impact for its seriousness. Many impact claims may be of wildly differing severity. Cancer and the common cold are both illnesses, but we would hardly say they were comparable.
    - *Analyze probability.* If the affirmative is claiming some future impact, it must indicate the probability of that event. Too often debaters evaluate scenarios as being 100% or 0%, when the reality is somewhere in between.
    - *Review time frame.* Traditionally, those events in the immediate future tend to dominate our attention, because we know more about them than those in the distant future. This is called "future discounting." Events that are coming sooner are often thought to be more important than events that happen later.

Thus, negative debaters should challenge affirmative scenarios for their time frame: "When will this happen and how long will it take?" This challenge alone may not defeat a scenario, but it may make the negative's arguments with a shorter time frame outweigh the affirmative scenarios.

- *Check for reversibility.* Traditionally, we think of reversible events as less important than irreversible because mistakes made in terms of reversible events can be repaired. Point out when out when affirmative scenarios are reversible while negative scenarios are not.

- *Weigh morality of the advantage.* You may be able to justify a quantitatively unfortunate situation because of the morally required actions involved. For example, parents would be unwilling to kill their child even if it was necessary for the betterment of the entire community. As well, slavery might be economically advantageous, but it would still be morally wrong.

- *Determine if the risk is voluntary.* Some situations, such as smoking, involve voluntary risk; others, such as being killed by a burglar, involve involuntary risk. If possible, argue that affirmative impact scenarios involve voluntary risk. While this argument will not eliminate the affirmative scenario, it might make it easy to outweigh the affirmative with negative scenarios that involve involuntary risks.

- *Compare the percentage to the total.* One way to make something seem small is to compare it to something big. For example, while 3% of a population affected by some malady is a notable impact scenario, it does not seem nearly as important as the 97% of the population that was untouched. This tactic, however, is only marginally effective and needs to be utilized in combination with others in this section.

- *Compare through time and space.* Descriptions of impact scenarios are always statements based on expectations and so are trapped in time and space. Use these comparisons to reduce the apparent magnitude of affirmative impact scenarios. For example, while things are not perfect, they may be (1) better than at any time in history, or (2) better than in any other country in the world.

ATTACKING AFFIRMATIVE SOLVENCY

The affirmative gets no credit for simply identifying the problem, only solving it. You probably won't be able to prove that the plan will be completely useless, but you ought to make the affirmative's solvency as negligible as possible. Here are some basic techniques for attacking affirmative solvency:

- *Find the number in the solvency evidence.* Even the best affirmative solvency evidence will not claim to solve the problem completely. In fact, most affirmative teams can only find evidence that indicates that the plan will solve "some" or "much" of the problem. Point this out and start specifying amounts—the plan will only solve 30% of the problem, less than half of the problem, etc. Make the affirmative quantify its solvency, and if it can't suggest a high number with evidence, you should suggest a low number.
- *Attack specific approaches.* The affirmative will use a specific technique to solve a problem. Use evidence indicating that this approach is not effective.
- *Attack the solvency evidence.* Often the affirmative will find an example of a plan that worked locally and advocate applying it nationally. Any time the affirmative tries to generalize from a small example, you can attack its solvency.
- *Find alternative causes.* Most problems have multiple causes. Find those alternative causes and show how the affirmative's plan does not address them.
- *Find ways for people to sabotage the plan.* If the affirmative inherency is that people don't like or don't want the plan, then they will try to sabotage it. To create this argument, first find a reason why people will want to sabotage the plan and then find a way for them to sabotage it.

Conclusion

Don't let them win the case without a debate! Keep arguing no matter what!

Attack the affirmative case explicitly and immediately. This will gain you a refutational advantage as well as demonstrate the kind of clash that so many judges are looking for. Familiarize yourself with the techniques above. They can make your attack far more effective.

Exercises

1. Train yourself to use challenges effectively. Take your first affirmative speech, another speech, or even a newspaper or magazine editorial and read it carefully. Develop effective challenges. Don't take too much time—in a debate you need to think quickly. Follow the pattern of inadequacy and implication discussed in this section. Deliver these challenges aloud to practice your speaking and word economy.

2. List all the harms that an affirmative team could argue on a given topic. Prioritize them based on which harms you think the affirmative would most likely use. Write one of these on the top of a sheet of paper and then develop arguments against it using the guidelines in this section. Carefully word your arguments and practice. When you finish one harm, move on to the next.

3. Make sample arguments against popular affirmative cases explaining how the affirmative's position on inherency can be used against it.

4. After each tournament, create a sheet of negative solvency arguments for each affirmative case that you debated. You will repeat some arguments, so pay special attention to developing these effectively. Organize these notes for the next time you debate that team.

5. During tournaments get the citation for the solvency evidence that the affirmative team used. Research this evidence and study it care-

fully. Often you can discover powerful arguments to use against the affirmative. Prepare these for the next time you meet that particular team.

6. Hold a practice debate that is just about the affirmative case, with no use of other types of arguments. Often case arguments are not developed in enough depth in a single debate, but by having a practice debate that focuses only on case arguments, you can become adept at using them to your advantage.

4

The Disadvantage

The affirmative will talk about the benefits of its plan, and so the negative must address the ways in which the plan would cause specific disadvantages. Disadvantages (also called "disads" or "Das") are most often negative arguments that prove the effects of the plan would be bad. Thus, debaters compare the disadvantages of a proposal to the advantages of a proposal to decide whether the effects of the plan are more advantageous than disadvantageous.

Components

Most disadvantage arguments have the following components:

Title: what you want to call the argument in the debate. A descriptive title like "The plan will cause unemployment" can be useful.

Thesis: a concise version of the entire argument. Present the thesis first so that the judge is familiar with the basic argument before you go into detail. The thesis acts very much like a topic sentence in a paragraph—it alerts the judge as to what is to come.

Links: reasons why adopting the affirmative's plan would cause the disadvantage. It should include why the affirmative is responsible for

the disadvantage. The link states why the affirmative plan causes the problem, or at least sets in motion a chain of causality that results in a problem. The negative often supports its argument by reading a piece of evidence.

Internal Links: other logical connections needed to reach the final step, proving how very bad the result will be. Sometimes when the plan changes something, it does not cause a problem right away. The internal link states that when the plan causes something to change, which is the link, this can lead to an intervening step, and then that causes the problem, which is the impact. For example, a proposal may cost a lot of money (link), and this may cause other programs to be cut (impact), but you need an internal link to establish that programs will be cut instead of taxes or deficit spending being increased.

Impact: describes the problem that will result and explains how very harmful it will be. The impact is usually something that we would all agree is a serious thing that should be avoided. The negative uses this impact to claim that the affirmative plan should not be adopted because although the plan might cause some good things to happen, the disadvantages the plan leads to are much more important.

Types of Disadvantage Scenarios

When you are developing a disadvantage, you need to understand the different kinds of harm scenarios, because a disadvantage works differently depending on the event you are describing. The plan might result in a problem, or it might exacerbate an already existing problem, but both situations would be disadvantageous. Here are two different types of harm scenarios that a disadvantage might be describing.

THRESHOLD SCENARIO

The threshold scenario deals with events that either happen all at once or not at all. The threshold is how big the plan has to be to cause the problem presented in the disadvantage. Thresholds are either high or low. For example, China has a close economic relationship with the United States, and the United States would have to do something pretty serious to damage it. The United States often criticizes China's human rights record without eliciting any reaction from China. However, if the United States were to covertly fund Chinese human rights organizations and require that all Chinese products carry a sticker warning people that the product came from a society with a poor human rights record, China might retaliate. In this scenario the United States has taken serious action, and China may have reached its high threshold of tolerance.

When addressing this type of scenario, you must show brink or uniqueness.

- *Brink.* The brink argument states that there is a risk of a problem happening at some point in the future. In the China example it took something very serious to potentially damage relations with the United States.

- *Uniqueness.* The uniqueness argument states that without the plan there will be no problem, but with the plan there will be. In our example, the negative disadvantage must show that relations with China are good now but will be damaged by the plan of funding human rights groups and labeling Chinese products. The damage done to U.S.–Chinese relations takes place only if the plan is adopted; thus the disadvantage is "unique" to the plan.

Falling Off a Cliff—Understanding Threshold Scenarios

We can illustrate the components of a disadvantage and the concept of brink and unique in threshold scenarios with the following example.

Falling off a cliff is a bad thing. Let's use that as a disadvantage.

You are standing near the edge of the cliff, and if you fall off, that would be a bad thing (a DISADVANTAGE).

If someone pushes you (LINK), then you would fall off the cliff.

If you fall off, you will hit the rocks below and get seriously injured (IMPACT).

If you are standing at the edge (BRINK: LOW THRESHOLD) of the cliff, just a little shove (LINK) will push you over.

If you are standing far back from the edge (BRINK: HIGH THRESH-OLD), a little push (LINK) won't send you over the edge, but a big shove (LINK) might.

If you would not fall off unless someone shoves you, then without a push you will remain safe (UNIQUE).

If you are already running toward the edge of the cliff, then an extra push won't make any difference (NOT UNIQUE), you are going to fall off no matter what.

If the fall is a long one and you land on sharp rocks, then the fall is a very bad thing (BIG IMPACT).

If the fall is a short one and you land on soft feather pillows, then it is not a bad thing (NO IMPACT).

LINEAR SCENARIO

A linear scenario deals with a harmful event already taking place that the affirmative plan makes worse or makes happen more frequently. For example, exposure to radiation is a linear event. All of us are exposed to radiation daily, but the more radiation we are exposed to, the more harmful it is. You would show that the affirmative plan has a unique link to exposing us to more radiation by, for example, disposing of toxic nuclear waste in your school cafeteria.

In this situation you need to prove no brink or uniqueness, just a strong link. Since radiation exposure is happening now, and if more radiation exposure would be bad, and the affirmative causes more exposure to radiation, the affirmative plan makes an existing problem far worse. This is the essence of a linear harm scenario.

Structure of a Sample Disadvantage Argument

Most disadvantages begin with the link and end with the impact. In between other needed elements are added, such as internal link, brink, uniqueness, etc. Here is a simple example.

Name: Resource Trade-Off

Thesis: There are limited fiscal resources. When the affirmative requires that substantial additional resources must be directed at a certain program (preventive repair of bridges), then those resources will have to come from somewhere else. The political system will cut resources from an area that has a weak constituency and so can be cut with minimal political backlash. Programs for those in poverty have weak constituencies, so they will be cut. Thus, more resources for preventive bridge repair cause cuts in programs for the poor, such as welfare and food stamps.

  A. Affirmative mandates enormously expensive preventive repair of bridges. (LINK)
  B. There are limited resources, and new resources must be found by cutting programs with weak political constituencies. (INTERNAL LINK)
  C. When new resources are required, programs for the poor such as welfare and food stamps get cut first because they have weak political constituencies. (INTERNAL LINK)
  D. Cuts in programs for the poor will increase suffering as well as increase malnutrition, especially among children. (IMPACT)

Other Concepts You Might Find Useful

Construction and defense of disadvantage scenarios can be a complex exercise, but it is nevertheless very important if you, as the negative, want to win the debate. Here are two other considerations you might want to keep in mind.

The time frame is how long it takes for the onset of the problem that the disadvantage presents. If there is an especially short time frame, then the problem the plan creates might happen before whatever good things the plan creates. If that is the case, then the plan probably isn't a good one. If there is a long time frame, then the good things the plan creates would happen before the problems it creates. If this is the case, the plan probably is a good idea.

PREEMPTIONS

If you know that the affirmative is going to make a certain answer, you might want to anticipate it and insert a point denying that answer. When you anticipate an argument and answer it before it is made, debaters call that a preemption.

Advice to Affirmatives: How to Answer a Disadvantage

Every disadvantage is like a chain of reasoning. It starts with the link and ends with the impact. Like any chain, it is only as strong as its weakest link. You only need to break the chain at one critical point to defeat the disadvantage. Here are several ways you can do this. (The short name of the method is in parenthesis next to it.)

- *Disprove the link to your plan* (No link or link take-out). The link take-out states that the affirmative plan doesn't actually cause the problem the disadvantage presents. For example, you can argue that preventive bridge repair is not very expensive, or that it can be paid for through bonds or an increase in taxes. Thus, the plan for preventive bridge repair does not link to the disadvantage scenario.
- *Disprove impact* (No impact or impact take-out). The impact take-out states that the problem the disadvantage presents is not serious or harmful. For example, you can argue that welfare programs are not that valuable because the poor spend the money they receive on luxu-

ries and other items not necessary for livelihood. You could also claim that people are in poverty because of their own choices, and thus simply giving them money does not solve the problem but rewards poor decisions.

- *Disprove internal link* (No internal link or internal link take-out). Some needed logical step is missing or false. Explain this, and make sure to show that this step is critical to the entire disadvantage argument. For example, the government does not cut programs for weak political constituencies but cuts programs it thinks are wasteful. Programs for those in poverty do not fall into the later category. The government would cut other programs, such as agricultural price supports, instead.

- *Argue link turn.* Our policy actually solves this problem. Not to be used with impact turn. The link turn states that when the affirmative plan happens, the problem the disadvantage presents is avoided. This often means that when the affirmative plan happens, the exact opposite of the problem occurs. If the disadvantage is partially happening in the status quo, this answer will create a new advantage for the affirmative. For example, preventive bridge repair invigorates the transportation system necessary for economic growth as well as creating many new jobs. Thus, the plan creates additional tax revenues, so funding for the poor need not be cut.

- *Argue impact turn.* The thing we cause is not bad; it is actually good. Not to be used with link turn. The impact turn states that the problem the disadvantage presents is actually a good thing. For example, welfare and food stamp programs create a cycle of dependency that creates intergenerational poverty. Cuts in the welfare system would mobilize those currently in it to seek extra training and jobs, thus moving people from welfare to work. Cutting welfare programs in this way might be seen as a good thing.

- *Argue not intrinsic.* Other forces will intervene to stop the impact from taking place. For example, those policy makers and portions of the public who are concerned about the issue of poverty in the United

States would not allow these cuts to be made. Forces already in place will prevent the disadvantage from happening. Applies to policy system/plan of opponents as much as it does to us, so irrelevant.

The disadvantage may also apply to the counterplan of the negative, making it irrelevant for determining which to adopt. If the counterplan would have the states do the preventive bridge repairs and not the federal government, the disadvantage would still take place at the state level and the states would cut their poverty programs.

- *Argue no brink proven.* There is not enough of a link to push us over into impact X. We are now standing far back from the cliff edge, so the push the negative identifies (LINK) will not push us over the edge. For example, the affirmative might argue that the federal government has lots of money and will not cut programs for the poor unless it has no choice, because to do so would make them look bad to voters.
- *Argue not unique.* Will happen/should have happened anyway because of X. The non-unique argument states that the problem the disadvantage presents will happen anyway in the status quo. If it were to happen anyway, it doesn't matter if the affirmative plan causes the problem or not. For example, the affirmative can argue that welfare programs are already being cut and those formerly receiving benefits are already being pushed into the job market.
- *Argue case outweighs (bigger, sooner, etc.).* If the impact of the disadvantage would be smaller than the advantage of the plan, then even if the disadvantage were true, you would still adopt the plan. For example, the affirmative might argue that preventive bridge repair is more important than some cuts in welfare programs, because unless we fix the bridges our entire transportation system will break down.

Winning Disadvantages on the Negative

Even if a disadvantage is strong, you may mishandle it in the debate. To avoid that, keep these bits of advice in mind.

- *Deal with every one of the affirmative's answers.* To win the disadvantage, you have to defeat all affirmative answers.
- *Explain how the plan uniquely causes the impacts.*
- *Take special care to answer and defeat all turns.* These are especially dangerous, as they allow the affirmative to claim that the net effect of the disadvantage is to support the adoption of the plan.
- *Weigh impacts.* Show the judge that the disadvantage is greater than the advantages of the affirmative case.

Kicking Out of Disadvantages

Sometimes the affirmative has great answers to your disadvantage. Don't waste your time trying to win this disadvantage if the affirmative's answers are excellent. Instead, "kick out" of the disadvantage. Strategically concede it so that it is no longer in the debate and you can focus on better arguments. Here is a way to dispose of a disadvantage you would not like to continue arguing. Make sure you have considered all five of these elements when doing so. This list explains when you might want to kick out of a disadvantage and how you would go about doing that.

1. If the affirmative has great answers, don't waste your time . . . kick out of it.
2. Kick out explicitly. Tell the judge you are doing so, so you can focus on more important arguments. This leaves the impression that you are thinking strategically.
3. If you kick out of disadvantages with turns on them, you will lose. When the affirmative turns the disadvantage, it is an independent reason to vote for the affirmative. You can't just concede the disadvantage, or you will lose the debate. The negative team must never drop the turns on its disadvantage!

4. To kick out of disadvantages with turns on them, concede specific other affirmative responses that would make the turn irrelevant. For example, if the disadvantage is not true, it cannot be turned. Explain why conceding response X makes the turn irrelevant.

5. Conceding the "not unique" argument does not take out the link turn. Be careful in conceding "not unique" arguments to take out turns; logically it does not work. If the problem is going to happen no matter what, then we will actually need the plan's ability to turn the link (stop the problem) more than if it was unlikely to happen.

Exercises

1. After you have developed a disadvantage to use on a topic through research and strategizing, build the first negative version carefully. This is called your "shell," or the way you first present the argument. Have a longer and a shorter version, thus allowing you to allocate time more strategically. Develop a list of "links" (things that set the disadvantage in motion) that you can insert into the shell based on what the affirmative says and does in its plan.

2. After a tournament, examine all of the answers that affirmative opponents used against a disadvantage and prepare arguments dealing with each of these answers. Conduct research to locate evidence to support your arguments, or look carefully through the evidence that you already have to determine how to use it effectively. This exercise will make you better prepared to debate those particular teams the next time, and save you valuable preparation time.

3. As a member of the affirmative team, think about the disadvantages that the negative can make against your plan. Use the ideas in this chapter to draw up a list of answers to the argument or arguments. After a tournament, draw up new lists of answers to unexpected

disadvantages that negative teams used against you, and refine your previous lists.

4. Hold a practice debate that is only about a disadvantage. Often disadvantage arguments are not developed deeply in a single debate, but by having a practice debate that focuses solely on a disadvantage, you can become adept at using this issue to your advantage.

5

The Counterplan

Many people who are unfamiliar with modern policy debating think that the negative must defend the status quo. This is not true. The negative can claim that the status quo is indeed faulty but that the affirmative plan will not solve the problem and that the negative's counterplan, its rival proposal, will. Just like the affirmative's plan, the counterplan explains what the negative thinks should be done and how. The counterplan is almost always presented in the 1NC and then becomes the policy that the negative defends.

Criteria

After presenting its counterplan, the negative has a number of criteria to meet for the judge to weigh the advantage of the counterplan against the affirmative plan.

- *The counterplan must be non-topical.* Some judges require that the negative NOT embody the resolution in its proposal (the negative, after all, is supposed to "negate" the resolution, not "affirm" it). Non-topical in one word or term only is sufficient to show that the negative is not "affirming" the resolution. For example, you might offer a counterplan at the state level against an affirmative team with a proposal at the national level. Many judges accept topical counterplans if they are competitive (see below), because that is sufficient to divide argumentative ground in the debate in a fair way.

- *The counterplan has to be competitive.* The counterplan must be an alternative, not an addition to, the plan. It is competitive with the affirmative plan if it would be better to adopt just the counterplan instead of BOTH the affirmative plan and the counterplan.

    You can use several standard types of arguments to show that the counterplan is competitive. The strongest are the following:

    - *Mutual exclusivity competition*: the counterplan and the affirmative plan cannot coexist.
    - *Net benefits competition*: using the counterplan is better than using both the counterplan and the affirmative plan. Often having a disadvantage that applies to the affirmative plan that does not apply to the counterplan will illustrate this.

    Avoid the following—weaker—competitiveness arguments.

    - *Philosophical competition*: the philosophies behind the two are contradictory. Contradictory thoughts, of course, have never been a problem for some people, especially policy makers, so this standard is of little real use.
    - *Topical competition*: if the counterplan is not topical, the affirmative cannot adopt it. Wrong, the test is "substitution" of one for the other, not topicality.
    - *Redundancy*: there is no need to adopt both the plan and the counterplan, because adopting just the counterplan solves the problem. This is incorrect unless the counterplan has 100% solvency, which is difficult to imagine.

- *The counterplan must have an advantage.* It has to solve a problem or produce an advantage. The counterplan, therefore, must have significance and solvency, just like the affirmative case. The affirmative may argue that the counterplan has no advantage because it "doesn't work," but its advantage may be a disadvantage: it avoids a harm that the affirmative plan does not.

The counterplan may have disadvantages alleged against it by the affirmative, just as the negative alleges disadvantages against the affirmative plan.

The counterplan is often effectively used along with a disadvantage. If there is a disadvantage to the affirmative plan that does NOT apply to the counterplan, then that makes the counterplan net benefits competitive. This way the counterplan solves for the affirmative advantage, it may even have another advantage, and it also avoids the disadvantage that applies to the affirmative plan. This sort of integrated strategy can be very effective.

Example of Counterplan Debating: What Should We Do Tonight?

The arguments surrounding a counterplan seem complex and confusing, but like many debate concepts, once you apply them to everyday situations, they make a lot more sense. Let's use the example of what to do tonight.

1. The affirmative says that we should to go a movie tonight. That is the affirmative *plan*.
2. The negative counterplan is that we should not go to a movie but go out to dinner.
3. The affirmative responds that the counterplan is not competitive, because we can do both—go to dinner and then go to a movie (logical permutation).
4. The negative replies that we do not want to do both (logical permutation) because we cannot afford to do both (net benefits competition), but also we can't do both because dinner and the movie are at the same time (mutual exclusivity competition).
5. The affirmative replies that we do have enough money to do both (not net beneficial to do just the counterplan), and that we can go to dinner and then see a later showing of the movie (time permutation).
6. The negative finally explains that the disadvantage of going to the movie is that the movie is terrible, full of racism and sexism (disadvantage to the plan operating as a net benefits argument).

Answering Counterplans

Counterplans must meet certain burdens in order to defeat the affirmative plan; therefore, the affirmative must show why the counterplan does not meet these burdens. You can attack the counterplan in the following ways:

- *Attack topicality.* The counterplan cannot be accepted if it is topical because only the affirmative defends the resolution.
- *Attack competitiveness.* If we do not have to choose between the plan and the counterplan, then there is no reason to vote against the affirmative case. To show that the counterplan is not competitive, you can
  - *Prove that the plan and counterplan are not mutually exclusive.* We can do both at the same time.
  - *Prove it is not net beneficial.* We should do both at the same time.
  - *Offer permutations.* The affirmative generally answers competition with the permutation test. Permutations are arguments that prove the entire plan can be combined with parts of the counterplan in order to gain the advantages of the counterplan without rejecting the plan. It suggests ways in which the plan and counterplan could be merged to address the problem. If the affirmative shows that it can and should "do both," then the counterplan becomes irrelevant for the debate. Suggesting a permutation ("perm") of the counterplan does not indicate advocacy of it by the affirmative, just testing it for its relevance to whether we should see the counterplan as a reason to reject the affirmative plan or not. Here are the generally accepted types of permutations.
    - Logical permutation: do both at the same time.
    - Time permutation: do one first, then the other.
    - Partial permutation: do the counterplan everywhere except in the area of the affirmative plan.

    Do not use the following—weaker—types of permutations.
    - Restructuring permutation: change the plan in major ways so that it can be done at the same time as the counterplan.

Wrong. This involves an advocacy shift. The affirmative presented its plan and shouldn't be allowed to rework the plan just because it doesn't know how to answer the counterplan.

- Non-topical permutation: change the plan into something non-topical and then argue that the two can be done at the same time. Wrong. The affirmative still needs to be topical to win the debate.

- *Argue solvency.* Contend that the counterplan does not solve the problem. See if the counterplan solves the affirmative harms, provides advantages, and avoids the disadvantages. A counterplan that does not solve the problem the affirmative outlined has a clear solvency deficit.

- *Assert disadvantages.* Counterplans can have disadvantages. Argue that if the counterplan were accepted, something bad would happen that would not have happened if the affirmative plan had been adopted.

Exercises

1. Keep the flows (the notes debaters take during a debate) of counterplans used against you. Analyze the flows to determine if the counterplans do not compete or do not solve the problem your plan solves. Write your answers into a set of frontlines.

2. Think of a counterplan that was used against you. Develop a response strategy arguing only that the counterplan would have unique disadvantages that the affirmative plan does not have. Do some research to find interesting arguments that will take the negative by surprise.

3. Design a counterplan-disadvantage pair that you would use against a specific case. The counterplan must compete with the plan, must solve the problem, *and* have a disadvantage that is unique to the plan and does not link to the counterplan. This kind of integrated strategy can be very effective.

4. Hold a practice debate only on a counterplan. Often debaters do not develop counterplan arguments deeply in a single debate, but by having a practice debate that focuses only on a counterplan, you can become adept at using them.

6

The Process of Critique

Most of the arguments in a debate round are based on those made by traditional policy makers, such as legislators and political analysts. Increasingly, however, debaters have begun to model some of their arguments on the analyses of philosophers, rhetorical critics, and other scholars. This technique, the process of critique, often opens the debate up to new and exciting perspectives on traditional policy making that students find quite interesting and useful.

The critique—the kritik or the K—is an argument that focuses on the affirmative's language or assumptions rather than on the effectiveness of the plan. Sometimes the affirmative makes these assumptions by choice, and sometimes it makes these assumptions because it's the affirmative's job to defend the resolution. One of the simplest examples of a critique might be an argument that the language the affirmative uses is racist. For example, some scholars argue that certain kinds of policy language contain hidden racism, such as some of the arguments made against welfare. If the affirmative were to make one of these arguments, the negative might use a critique to point out the hidden racism in the case as a reason to vote against the affirmative.

Don't worry if you're confused. Critiques are complicated arguments, and many people are not familiar with the kinds of ideas associated with them, so let's answer some basic questions.

What is the critique? As you've learned, a critique is a way to criticize the assumptions an affirmative makes or the language debaters use to make their arguments. What is an assumption? An assumption is a part of an argument that people think is true but they never explicitly prove to be true.

How are assumptions revealed? Sometimes the language that we use to make our claims and arguments reveals our assumptions. Sometimes assumptions are revealed in the way we claim to know something or in the framework through which problems are analyzed. For example, often affirmatives assume that endless economic growth would be good or that nation X's increased power is advantageous. Look at the framework the other team uses to view the issues. Analyze the language it uses as well as the goals it seeks in order to reveal assumptions you may wish to critique.

How does the negative attack the assumptions? First, you must identify the assumption. Second, you must explain how the assumption links to the critique. Finally, you must explain the implications of the critique. For example, you might argue that

1. The affirmative claims that economic growth is always good;
2. The affirmative advantage is huge economic growth;
3. The implications of an unquestioning pursuit of economic growth can be quite harmful. For example, unregulated growth can cause serious environmental problems.

What are the possible implications of the critique? Generally, critiques can have three implications:

1. The critique might establish that the affirmative case does not prove the harm. For example, what is wrong with living a comfortable life versus a life of extravagance? Current living standards are hardly deprivation.
2. The critique might prove that the affirmative is unable to solve for its goal. A new car does not necessarily improve our life.

3. The critique might have consequences similar to those of a disadvantage. In other words, a critique would justify voting against
the affirmative altogether in order to reject the assumptions the
affirmative makes. If we focus just on money to buy "things," we
neglect the really important elements of our lives, such as family,
relationships, and meaningful work.

Here is an outline of a basic critique to show how you would present it
in the debate:

1. *The affirmative assumes X.* Mention specific language and arguments that reveal the assumption. "The affirmative assumes that
   limitless economic growth is beneficial."
2. *The assumption of X is not true.* Explain and prove your assertion.
   "Once we are living at some level of comfort, there is little value
   in having extra money and using it to buy extra things we do not
   really need. Money cannot buy happiness or love."
3. *Implications.*
   - The affirmative case does not prove the harm. "Given B, they
     cannot show that people do not have enough to live on com-
     fortably." (No harm)
   - The affirmative is unable to solve the problem it isolates. "More
     money will not make people any happier." (No solvency)
   - Consequences similar to those of a disadvantage. "Focus on
     money and additional commodities merely degrade our ap-
     preciation of more important things, like family and friends."
     (Harmful consequences)

The critique can operate in the simplest facets of your life. You witness
some of these in your own experience. Thinking about testing and test
taking can illustrate how a critique might function when the affirmative
proposes that testing play a larger role in American education. Here are
three possible implications of the critique:

1. *Challenging the harm assumptions.* Many people assume students do not learn as much as they used to because test scores are lower than they were in the past. However, the negative might challenge the assumption that test scores are a reliable measure of student achievement. This challenges the way proponents of testing assume test scores provide useful information. If the test scores are unreliable, then the affirmative cannot prove the harm by proving test scores are low. Test scores, the negative would argue, do not reveal accurate information of student achievement; therefore, they cannot be used to prove that students are underachieving.

2. *Challenging solvency.* Many people argue that testing should be used to guide curriculum changes in order to enhance student learning. However, if tests are critiqued because they do not truly measure what a student has learned, then using test results to revise the curriculum is a wasted exercise and will not achieve the goal of improving student achievement.

3. *Disadvantageous consequences.* The negative might argue that in light of the critique, there are disadvantage implications of supporting the affirmative. Some might argue that testing does not measure knowledge but instead indicates how good students are at taking tests. Many believe that tests are designed to discriminate in favor of the knowledge that upper-class whites are likely to have. Increasing tests or making tests more rigorous will only serve to perpetuate racism and sexism in education. The negative might argue that the judge should reject any policy that results in greater racism and sexism.

Why Are Critiques Valuable?

Critiques are valuable arguments for several reasons:

- *Critiques are highly generic.* They can be applied to a large variety of cases. The resolution always makes critical assumptions, and the critique provides a general argument you can use to attack the resolution.

Thus, in the example above, whenever an affirmative team opposing educational changes in its plan endorses testing, this argument can be used against the affirmative.

- *Critiques have multiple consequences.* They can minimize the affirmative advantage while also providing an argument to weigh against whatever advantage the affirmative claims. The critique of testing above is effective against the affirmative's harms, solvency, and plan.

- *Critiques integrate many arguments into one position.* Because the critique frequently applies to the affirmative case as well as the plan, the negative has a position in the debate that is coherent, as opposed to being composed of unrelated ideas. For example, the educational reform the affirmative proposes runs into the critique of testing at almost every level of its presentation.

- *Critiques frequently have* a priori *implications.* An *a priori* argument must be resolved first, usually before the substantive issues of the debate are resolved. In our example of testing, the negative could argue that policies that reinforce racism or sexism are so evil that they need to be avoided absolutely. If testing is racist or sexist, it should be rejected regardless of substantive benefits that might result from increased testing.

- *Critiques frequently avoid uniqueness problems.* Affirmative debaters frequently rely on some element of the current system to implement its plans or to prove why new policies would better achieve the goals of the present system. Critique authors frequently argue, in effect, that the goals of the present system should be rejected at every opportunity. If the arguments against testing were presented as a disadvantage, the affirmative could claim that we already use testing (not unique) in education at almost every level, so the affirmative does not, on balance, increase testing as an important part of the educational system. But with a critique the situation is somewhat different. For example, if testing is wrong then we should reject it every time we find it. In addition, many critique authors argue that the most important place to reject accepted ideas is in individual settings, such as a debate, thus making the critique unique each time a judge has the opportunity to reject the affirmative.

- *Critiques shift the debate to negative ground.* Affirmatives are used to debating on their ground: the case evidence and the implications of the plan. Critiques offer negatives the opportunity to shift the focus of the debate to an issue they are more familiar with: the intricacies of the critique. This can give the negative an advantage in the round. For example, in our example above, instead of talking about the affirmative's issues of student achievement, the debate can be moved to negative ground by discussing the ways in which achievement is measured and determined.

Types of Critiques

Michael Bryant, director of forensics at Weber State University in Utah has argued that there are five different types of critiques/kritiks emerging from competitive use:

1. *Critiques of Knowing.* The affirmative may claim that they "know" something quite definitely, or they may say something that violates a specific philosophical school (contemporary postmodernism, for example, which argues that when we believe we "know" things, we are setting ourselves up for failure because all knowledge is fragmentary and disconnected) and thus they cannot be said to really "know" or "prove" anything, thus losing the debate. For example, we may think that we "know" about the Gulf War of 1990–1991, but all we really know is what we were told in the media in the construction of a meta-reality. To think that we actually "know" what happened as fact and knowledge is a dangerous idea.

2. *Foundation Critiques.* These arguments attempt to broaden the scope of the weighing process, the process by which the judge determines which arguments are more important, by examining assumptions undergirding positions. Advocacy is built on assumptions, and when

those assumptions are disproven, the advocacy falls. For example, an argument may be built on the assumption that economic growth is a good thing and that we should pursue it. In actuality, economic growth may be harmful because it involves environmental destruction, a widening of resource disparities and a focus on commodities as the ultimate values in human existence, which is untrue based on experience.

3. *Inability.* This type of argument also examines the underlying nature of assumptions but results in advocacy to the judge in favor of rejecting weighing processes suggested by the affirmative due to inherent limitations on our ability to understand the full nature of uncovered forces or assumptions. For example, an individual employing this type of argument might suggest that we are all so engulfed and immersed in the commodification of time, space, and thought caused by global capitalism that we are incapable of accurate assessments of the benefits and drawbacks of such a system. Though some might claim this to be a priori, a better conclusion might be that the judge is asked to reject the very futility of weighing assessments when it becomes clear that such an attempt will be distorted by preexisting conceptual baggage that cannot be removed. In other words, the judge is asked to look at the weighing procedure and conclude that the effort is futile.

4. *Framework Critiques.* This type of argument states that the "lens of perception" or the "way of understanding" that the affirmative uses is false. For example, the affirmative view of foreign policy and international relations could be one of power politics. The negative could then argue that this is a false view of the way nations operate.

5. *Language Critiques.* Sometimes affirmatives are not careful about how they use language. Sexist, racist, homophobic, violent, and other forms of questionable language can be attacked in the critique. Based on the idea that "language creates reality" and the only real thing that is happening in the debate is "what we are all saying," the negative can argue that the affirmative should lose the debate. The judge

would not consider those who used this type of language to have done the "better job of debating."

Answering Critiques

While critiques are valuable negative arguments, they are also vulnerable to some general affirmative responses. You can use the following arguments against critiques. Make sure to adapt them to the specific critique you are addressing.

- *Attack the perspective the critique offers.* For example, you might argue that power politics (also known as realism) is the best way to understand how nations interact and the most effective view that policy makers can use.

- *Defend the assumption.* The assumption you have made may well be true and worthy of support. For example, we should adopt a realist view of international relations because that is how international policy makers view international relations.

- *Argue that you do not support the assumption the negative has identified.* What you have said and done is not a representation of this assumption, but of a completely different assumption that the negative has not attacked and that you may wish to defend. This way you disprove the link of the critique to your advocacy. For example, if an affirmative advocates increased development assistance to Africa, the negative might offer a critique that the role of women in development is usually ignored and as a result development efforts help men at the expense of women, which is a bad thing. The affirmative might respond that their development assistance programs reach both men and women in the same ways, thus not operating to further disadvantage women.

- *Note that the assumption is found everywhere in our world.* If a certain assumption is prevalent in human society, rejecting that assumption in one small domain means nothing when we move on to the next domain. The critique applies to everything, not just to your proposal, and thus is not an independent reason to reject your advocacy. For example, an affirmative argues in favor of tracking (putting students at similar academic performance levels together), and the negative critique argues that this is unacceptable because it treats different students differently and thus violates the standard of equality for students. The affirmative can respond that every student gets a different grade, a different class schedule, and a different desk, thus everything about the educational system already treats each student differently, so there is no reason to reject the proposal because of unequal treatment.

- *There is no alternative.* Often critiques will assert that a certain way of doing things (commodity-based life, capitalism, etc.) is bad. To support its argument the negative must demonstrate that there is an alternative. For example, it may indict capitalism, but to do so the negative needs to propose and defend a better alternative.

- *Attack the negative's alternative, if it has one.* Show that its alternative is every bit as bad if not worse than your proposal. For example, if an affirmative plan treats men and women differently, the negative might argue that the proposal uses current gender roles, and that the alternative of a unisex or genderless society would be better. The affirmative might attack this alternative as unrealistic because of physical differences between men and women that necessitate different treatment, as in childbearing and breastfeeding.

- *Contrast practical benefits of affirmative with philosophical implications of the critique.* The affirmative argues that it will adopt a policy change and that this policy change will have clear benefits. The negative argues against the affirmative in an often-philosophical way that may lack the tangibility and importance of the plan's immediate benefits. Judges can be urged to be "realistic" in voting against a critique, and called "responsible" because they help specific groups of people by backing the plan. For example, if the affirmative plan provides jobs to those who need them to support their families, that very real and actual need might outweigh less tangible negative claims that capitalist-based "work" has little value. In other words, telling that to the unemployed would not persuade them that they should not have jobs.

Exercises

1. List the most common assumptions likely to be made on the topic you are debating. Indicate which assumptions you believe are problematic and begin investigating them.

2. Make a list of the underlying assumptions behind several magazine advertisements. Select an assumption that you find problematic and use the critique process to disprove it. Then indicate why this product or service might be a bad choice given that the assumption is false.

3. Compile a list of assumptions that you may be making in your own affirmative case. Think about how to make your case without these assumptions or else prepare to defend them.

4. Whenever a team offers a critique against your affirmative case, spend some time during the next week writing answers to it. File them away for use the next time you debate.

5. Keep a record of the answers that the affirmative uses against your critiques and the responses you used to defend them. File them away for future use.

6. Hold a practice debate that is just about a critique. Often critique arguments are not developed deeply in a single debate, but by having a practice debate that focuses only on a critique, you can become adept at using this issue to your advantage.

7

The Topicality Argument

Debate is about making good policy, and you can't have a good policy unless you know what the key words of the policy mean. Some words are very difficult to define, and there are huge debates about them. How do you define "good" or "bad," for example? It's easy to understand this problem by thinking about a conversation you might have with your parents. Let's say your parents tell you to be home "at a reasonable hour." When you show up at 2:00 a.m., you get in big trouble. "But I was home at a reasonable hour," you complain. "All my friends stay out until 4:00." Your parents are not impressed. "Reasonable means midnight," they say. How were you supposed to know what "reasonable" meant? Topicality deals with arguments about what words mean.

Every year high school or university policy debate uses a different topic or resolution. The affirmative must develop specific policies (plans) that support the topic or resolution. That is the affirmative's assignment in the debate. If it does not fulfill that assignment, the affirmative will lose the debate. For example, your history teacher asked you to write a paper about the Civil War. You, however, decided to write a paper about the Vietnam War. Your history teacher might very well give you a grade of "F" because that wasn't the assignment. Likewise, the affirmative is assigned to write a case about the topic, and if it doesn't, the affirmative loses the debate. But it isn't usually that simple. You might tell your history teacher that your paper was about why the Vietnam War was like the Civil War and that the Vietnam War can teach us about the Civil War. If you made that argument well, you might not flunk the assignment. Likewise, even affirmatives with cases that don't seem to be about the topic often have a reason why they are topical.

Another way to understand topicality is to think of the topic as a contract. Professional sports stars know that they have to fulfill their contract if they want to get paid. If they violate any part of the contract, they may not get paid. The affirmative has to meet every part of the topic, every part of the contract, in order to win. If the negative can show that the affirmative failed, the negative can win the debate.

Arguing about Definitions

Of course, most affirmative plans seem topical at first. However, if you research different definitions for the words in the resolution, you may find definitions that contradict those the affirmative used. For example, suppose the resolution says we should increase aid to African nations? The affirmative might offer a plan to increase aid to Egypt. Is Egypt an African nation? Many people might say yes, since Egypt is on the continent of Africa. Many experts might say no, however, because Egyptian culture can be considered Middle Eastern instead of African. There is no right or wrong answer for what a word means, but it is possible to make arguments about which definition is better. If the negative's argument—that "Egypt" is not "Africa"—wins, then it may win the debate on the issue of topicality.

Winning with Topicality

Topicality exists to limit what the affirmative may talk about so the negative can have a reasonable chance to argue against the case. If the affirmative could talk about anything, how could the negative prepare for the debate? The negative argues that topicality is a voting issue, the issue that will determine the judge's decision in the debate. In other words, the negative argues that the affirmative should lose the debate if it can prove that the affirmative plan does not support the topic. You can win the debate by talking about definitions alone!

Topicality is a very powerful argument, because the affirmative can lose the debate on topicality, even if it is winning every other argument in the debate! After all, if the plan does not address the resolution, then who cares how great an idea it is? The judge would throw out all the affirmative arguments, just like a judge in a courtroom would throw out a case if it is irrelevant. Likewise in a debate, the judge cannot vote for a non-topical plan, because it is not in her jurisdiction.

Making a Topicality Argument

You can write topicality arguments before the debate. In general, topicality arguments have the following format:

- *Definition of the word or phrase in dispute.* Evidence that defines one or more important words in the resolution.
- *Violation of definition.* An explanation of why the affirmative plan is not an example of the kind of action described by the resolution. The explanation answers the question "Why does the plan violate the negative definition(s)?"
- *Reasons to prefer the negative definition.* Arguments about why the negative definition is better for debate than other definitions of the word(s) being contested. If the affirmative offers a different definition, why should the judge prefer the negative definition?
- *Voting issue.* Reasons why the affirmative should lose if the negative wins topicality. The two main reasons are jurisdiction and debatability. Jurisdiction means that the judge cannot vote for the plan if it is not part of the topic. Debatability, also known as reasonability, means

that the negative would not have a fair chance in the debate if the affirmative did not have to operate within the limits of the resolution.

Reasons to Prefer the Negative Definition(s)

Negatives use two types of arguments to prove their definitions are better than the affirmatives': standards and specific arguments.

Standards are very general arguments about definitions. They explain why one interpretation of a word or phrase is superior to another. Many negatives argue that definitions that draw a "bright line" are best. These definitions make it clear what is topical and what is not. For example, if I wanted to find a definition of the word "apple," I would not use one that defined it as "a fruit." That definition does not draw a bright line between apples and all other fruit. I would want a definition that distinguished apples from other kinds of fruit. There are hundreds of possible standards for definitions: more precise definitions are best, definitions that reflect common use are best, definitions that come from legal sources are best, and many more.

Specific arguments talk about the negative definition in the context of the resolution or the debate round. If the resolution is about computers, for example, I might argue that the word "apple" should mean "a specific brand of computer," instead of "a fruit," because the first definition is more specific to the other words in the resolution.

Specific arguments might also include arguments about grammar. For example, some words can be nouns or verbs. A specific topicality argument might assert that one of the words in the resolution should be defined in a certain way because it is used as a noun and not a verb. A person can possess a basic "right" (noun), but a person can also "right" (verb) a wrong that was done. Like standards, there are hundreds of possible specific arguments.

Remember, to win topicality, the negative must prove that

1. the negative definition is superior *and*
2. the affirmative plan does not meet the negative's definition.

Topicality Can Help with Other Arguments

You can also use topicality arguments to help set up and make your other arguments more credible. Very often negative arguments like disadvantages focus on some action phrase in the topic, since the negative can predict that the action specified in the topic will be used in affirmative plans. For example, if the topic calls for "increased foreign aid to Africa," the negative can prepare arguments that foreign aid is bad. Quite often affirmative teams try to structure their plans so that they do not necessarily use this action mechanism in the topic (foreign aid), thus allowing them to escape from the negative disadvantages about the harms of acting in that way by claiming that they "do not use the term foreign aid." By launching a topicality argument that claims that this required action element (foreign aid) does not exist in the plan and then also arguing that this action element (foreign aid) would be disadvantageous, the negative can catch the affirmative in a dilemma: if the affirmative takes the action called for in the topic, then the disadvantage comes about, and if it does not, it is not topical. Even if you do not win the topicality argument, the affirmative will, in answering it, have to explain how it does, indeed, take this action (foreign aid), which creates the link to the disadvantage for you. To prove that it is topical, the affirmative will have to prove that its plan is, indeed, "foreign aid," and thus the disadvantage will apply.

Answering Topicality

Don't panic! Just because the negative makes an argument, don't assume that it's true. Winning topicality is very difficult for the negative and relatively easy for the affirmative. Don't get cocky, though. If you're not careful, topicality can ruin an otherwise successful affirmative round.

AFFIRMATIVE TOPICALITY TIPS

Even if you think that your plan is clearly topical, do not be surprised if the negative makes the argument. It is a strategy the negative can engage in that costs it little (the negative cannot lose the debate because it said you were not topical), but the strategy can have a big reward for the negative (it might win the debate) if you answer it poorly. Affirmative teams must answer topicality arguments thoroughly. Here are some basic tips for answering topicality arguments.

- *Write your plan with an eye toward topicality.* When you write your affirmative case, you make a series of strategic decisions, most of which revolve around solving the problem your case identifies. Usually, you try to find the most effective policy for solving the problem. You should also look for a policy that seems to be a clear example of the resolution. Does the plan sound like it takes the kind of action required by the resolution? Write the plan using as many of the words in the resolution as possible.
- *Research the words of the resolution.* The negative will research various definitions of the important words in the resolution. You should do the same. Look for definitions that clearly include the kind of action the plan takes. Failing that, look for the broadest possible definitions.
- *Research contextual evidence.* If you show that experts define a term the same way you do, you can read that evidence to counter the negative's topicality argument and make your case sound reasonable.
- *Remember that advantages don't make you topical.* Topicality focuses on what the plan does. The fact that your advantages talk about the same things as the resolution is largely irrelevant to the issue of topicality. You must make sure that your plan is topical.
- *Prepare your topicality answers ahead of time.* Anticipate the kinds of topicality arguments the negative is likely to present, and write out answers and counter-definitions before the tournament.

COMMON RESPONSES TO TOPICALITY ARGUMENTS

Below are some possible responses to topicality arguments. Offer several different types of answers so that if one fails, the others may rescue you. Remember, the affirmative can lose the debate just on topicality, so you must make very sure that you have more than one way to answer the negative's topicality argument.

- *Present counter-definitions.* When the negative defines a word in the resolution so that your plan sounds non-topical, respond with a different definition of the same word that makes your plan sound topical. Once you present a counter-definition, make additional arguments about why your definition is better than the negative's.
- *Present contextual evidence.* Reading evidence from the topic literature that links your plan with the words of the resolution can help make your plan sound reasonable.
- *Present the "we meet" answer.* Read the negative's definition. Usually it isn't as exclusive as the negative says it is. Think of reasons your plan actually meets the negative's definition. In other words, think of reasons why the negative's definition actually describes your plan, instead of excluding it.
- *Point out how your interpretation does not distort the debate process.* The negative might try to argue that the plan is "abusive," that if the judge allows this plan to be topical, hundreds of other plans will also become topical. This is abusive because it puts too much of a burden on the negative to research those hundreds of new plans. You can counter with the following:
  - *Literature checks abuse.* Argue that your plan is not abusive because it is based on evidence found in the topic literature.
  - *Other words check abuse.* For example, "aid" may be a broad term, but the phrase "foreign aid" has a fairly specific meaning.
  - *Solvency checks.* The affirmative has to prove that its plan solves the problem that the case identified. You can often counter a topicality argument by arguing that its definitions could not really add

hundreds of new plans to the topic because most of the new plans would not solve the problem.

- *Present counter-standards.* The negative assumes that the judge must use certain standards to decide the issue of topicality. You should develop your own standards. The most common affirmative counter-standard is "reasonability." The affirmative argues that as long as the plan is reasonable, the judge should ignore topicality. You must provide reasons why your plan is reasonable. For example, you might say, "if the negative has evidence against the case—that is, if the negative can fairly debate the case—then the plan is reasonably topical." Even if the negative has a conflicting definition, the one the affirmative is using may very well be reasonable. You do not necessarily need to have the best definition in the debate: your definition only has to be reasonable.

REASONS WHY TOPICALITY IS NOT A VOTING ISSUE

Most debaters are taught that topicality is an absolute voting issue, which means that the negative can win the round just by winning topicality. Not everyone agrees. Here are three common reasons affirmatives give as to why the judge should not consider topicality:

- *Language is indeterminate.* Is there such thing as "the best" definition? Ultimately, the words we use to describe things are not precise. Because language is imprecise (or "indeterminate"), many affirmatives argue that it is unfair to base a decision on competing definitions. The use of a word is usually determined by the user. To say that the affirmative should lose the debate because it did not use the definition the negative preferred would be far too drastic. When someone uses a word in conversation that you do not understand, you would ask them to define it and then continue listening, not disagree with them and refuse to pay attention.
- *Topicality is not "real world."* Affirmatives can argue that topicality does not reflect the real world of policy making, in which issues are discussed broadly without narrow constraints of topicality.

- *Topicality silences important voices.* Affirmatives can argue that topicality is just another meaningless procedure that prevents important ideas from being debated. Arguments describing the importance of the plan are helpful in making this claim.

Ultimately, learning to debate the meaning of words and phrases can be very important later in life. Understanding the issue of topicality will help you in careers such as business, education, and law.

Exercises

1. Take the topic you are given and browse a variety of dictionaries. Find definitions for all the major words, read them carefully, and make a distinction between those definitions that are "broad" (useful for the affirmative because they leave the affirmative lots of flexibility) and "narrow" (useful for the negative because they leave the affirmative very little flexibility). Think about which definitions support your affirmative case and prepare to use them when the negative team argues topicality. Build a file of definitions for use on both sides of the topic.

2. List the affirmative cases you can expect to debate. Prioritize them in terms of which ones you will be most likely to debate and prepare topicality violations for use against them.

3. Hold a practice debate that is just about topicality. Often topicality arguments are not developed in depth in a single debate, but by having a practice debate that focuses on topicality, you can become adept at it to your advantage.

8

Debate Steps

A debate is composed of a number of speeches presented in a specific order. Each speech plays a different role in the process. In a debate competing pulses of information not only establish arguments but also criticize, rebuild, and defend them.

This chapter describes the purpose of each speech in the debate and offers tips on how you can present it effectively. Please do not read only the information on the speeches you will be giving. Take the time to read all suggestions so that you understand how you should respond to what others have done.

First Affirmative Constructive (1AC)

The 1AC begins the debate and presents the affirmative case. 1AC differs from all other speeches in the debate because it usually is completely scripted before the debate.

Tips

- *Be prepared.* Have your speech written out and well organized. Time it in advance so that you know how long it takes you to read it. Practice it so that you can deliver it properly. When you practice it, deliver it as if you really care about the issues. Debate is a game and a show, and when you put on a good show, you are more likely to win the game.

- *Be complete.* Make sure you address all the requirements: read the topic, address the stock issues (significance, inherency, plan, and solvency). Make sure that each of your contentions (your major issues) has evidence that proves the arguments.
- *Be strategic.* Write your plan so that it avoids or answers popular arguments that will be made against it. Anticipate what the negative might say and include evidence that answers these arguments. Presenting evidence here makes the 2AC's job easier.
- *Be ready to defend your speech in cross-examination.* Make sure you understand the evidence and can explain why your arguments are correct.
- *Carry a second copy of your speech in case the negative asks for it.*

First Negative Constructive (1NC)

In this speech the negative attacks the affirmative case and also spells out the major negative issues.

Tips

- *Don't use too much preparation time.* Prepare your disadvantages, critique, counterplan, and/or topicality arguments in advance so you can spend prep time on specific case attacks and challenges. You will need prep time later in the debate, so save it for then.
- *Make sure each major argument is logically complete.* Your disadvantages need links and impacts; your topicality arguments need definitions, violations, and voting issue; your counterplan needs to address topicality, competitiveness, advantage, and solvency. If your arguments do not have all of the necessary components, they may not make sense to the judge.

- *Watch time allocation.* Know how long it takes you to read each of your off-case arguments, the arguments you have prepared in advance. Practice and time them. Pace yourself as you speak so you don't fall behind or get too far ahead.
- *Make sure to attack the case.* Use a mixture of challenges and evidenced arguments to keep the affirmative team focused on the case so that the affirmative cannot spend all of its time answering your off-case arguments. Make sure to attack the affirmative's impact scenarios and solvency. Judges expect you to "clash" with the affirmative's case and you need to do so.
- *Be ready to defend your speech in cross-examination.* When the affirmative asks questions, use the opportunity to explain and elaborate on your arguments. Be able to defend them as well as explain them.

Second Affirmative Constructive (2AC)

2AC is one of the most difficult speeches in the debate. If you mishandle any of the important negative arguments, you may end up losing the debate, since this is the last constructive speech, and you will not be allowed to introduce new answers or arguments in the rebuttals.

Tips

- *Use your partner to help during her cross-examination of 1NC.* If you don't understand an issue, you won't be able to answer it. Have your partner ask questions about arguments you don't understand or the ones that seem the strongest against your case so that you can prepare your answers.
- *Answer every negative issue.* You cannot win the debate if you fail to answer an off-case argument like topicality, a disadvantage, a counterplan, or a critique. Prepare good answers for each one.
- *Answer the negative's arguments; don't explain them over again.* Explaining its arguments is the negative's duty, not yours. Your duty is to

answer them. Don't waste time telling the judge what the negative's arguments are about. The best way to save time is to tell the judge which argument you are answering ("On their counterplan, my answers are . . .") and then present your answers.

- *Number your answers to off-case arguments.* On a negative disadvantage, for example, tell the judge you are going to answer that disadvantage, and then number the answers as 1, 2, 3, etc. This will make it easy for the judge to differentiate your arguments, and set the stage for you and your partner to use specifically numbered arguments later in the debate ("The negative never comes to grips with my 5th answer, that . . ."). Judges love it when the 2AC numbers well.
- *Don't forget to defend the case.* You will probably need the case to win, so don't get bogged down in the off-case arguments. Spend at least as much time on the case as the negative did.
- *Use the 1AC evidence.* You included good evidence in your 1AC, so you could use it in 2AC. Refer to it and save time by not having to read it.
- *Think offense.* Obviously, you have to defend yourself against negative attacks, but make sure to mount an offense against the negative as well. Turn the negative's disadvantages and critiques, and offer disadvantages against its counterplans. Your offense puts the negative on the defensive. If you merely defend, the opposition is likely to break through at some point, but if you go on the offense against its arguments, you have more ways to win.
- *Be prepared.* Have prepared answers (frontlines) to arguments you expect or have heard before. Make them clear and quick to read, practice them, and edit them so that you can offer a lot of good responses to the negative's arguments.
- *Deal with voting issues.* Sometimes the negative will make an argument that it claims is a "voting issue"; it claims it can win the debate on this one argument. This is usually not the case. When the negative calls something a voting issue, make sure to respond to it specifically and disprove that claim.

- *Watch your time allocation.* Think about what you need to do in your speech and pace yourself. If you have 8 minutes, try to have completed 25% of your task in the first 2 minutes, 50% in the first 4 minutes, etc. Have your partner signal you about your time allocation.
- *Think on your feet.* While you are speaking, think of new answers to negative arguments that you did not write on your flowsheet, the paper you use to track arguments in a debate. Use those answers, but make sure to get them from your partner after your speech so that you can remember them for later.

Second Negative Constructive (2NC)

The negative focuses its attack in this speech. While the 1NC offered a number of arguments and issues, the next two negative speeches focus on developing and explaining them in more detail.

Tips

- *Divide the labor.* The 2NC and the 1NR occur back to back, so you need to divide up the issues in the debate. *The 2NC and the 1NR should never cover the same ground.* Dividing the labor maximizes your attack on the affirmative and puts a lot of pressure on the 1AR, which can make mistakes that could allow you to win.
- *Be complete.* You need to deal with *every* answer the 2AC makes to your arguments. If she has five answers to your disadvantage, you need to deal with all five. Emphasize the best answers.
- *Read evidence.* Now is your chance to really develop your arguments. Have the 10 best pieces of evidence ready to use before you speak. You may not read them all, but make sure they are available.
- *Complete your argument development.* The shell of the argument presented in 1NC isn't enough to win you the debate. You need to develop your arguments further, especially the impacts. You should always read extra impact evidence for your most important arguments.

- *Toss out your weak arguments.* Don't waste your time trying to defend the arguments the affirmative answers best: invest your time in the arguments for which its answers are weak. Strategically concede counterplans by conceding competition; strategically concede disadvantages as suggested in Chapter 4. You will be rewarded if you show the judge you are discarding your weak arguments and emphasizing your strong ones.
- *Don't drop the turns.* A good 2AC will try to turn your arguments, and in so doing will make them a new reason for voting for the affirmative. Don't let her do that. Defeating turns is your top priority. Then you can go on to win the argument.
- *Take advantage of affirmative mistakes.* If the affirmative does not emphasize a major issue, like a disadvantage or a critique, then you should focus in on that argument and really develop it. Make sure the judge knows that the few 2AC answers are all she can give—no new answers in rebuttals! If she drops a major argument, begin your speech with that and emphasize how the debate IS ALREADY OVER because of her error.
- *Watch for contradictions and double-turns.* Affirmative teams often get in trouble by trying to give too many answers, and at some point they begin to contradict themselves. Point this out. In the case of trying to turn both the link ("The affirmative solves this problem") and the impact ("This is not a bad thing, but actually a good thing") of a disadvantage, the affirmative merely creates a new reason why it should lose the debate. Judges love to vote negative on double-turns.
- *Weigh the issues.* Don't wait until the end of the debate to explain why your arguments are more important than the negative's. Begin the process in this speech, contrasting why your negative disadvantages and critiques are more important than the affirmative's case advantages. Remember to read more impact evidence.

First Negative Rebuttal (1NR)

This speech continues the work of the 2NC.

Tips

- *Don't take any prep time.* You had the 2NC prep time, the 2NC time, and the cross-examination of the 2NC time to prepare. That should be enough. Remember, if you take prep time for the 1NR, then the 1AR is also prepping during that time, and is *stealing your prep time*. Don't let the affirmative do that. Stand up immediately after the cross-examination of the 2NC and give your speech.
- *Divide the labor.* The 2NC and 1NR occur back to back, so you need to divide up the issues in the debate. As you just learned, this division maximizes your attack on the affirmative and puts pressure on the 1AR. Don't repeat what the 2NC has said—that just makes the job of the 1AR easier. If you divide the issues and cover each in more depth, you make the job of the 1AR far more difficult.
- *Follow all the guidelines for the 2NC.* So that you develop issues and put the 1AR in a difficult situation.

First Affirmative Rebuttal (1AR)

The goal of the 1AR is simple: don't lose the debate. The strategy is equally simple: don't drop any important issue. Cover every important argument. You cannot answer each subpoint on an argument, but you should answer any argument that could potentially win the debate for the negative. There are three areas in which you may drop some subpoints on an issue but still address the entire issue:

1. *Disadvantages.* Pick a set of 2AC arguments to extend. For example, use answers 2, 4, and 6 on the disadvantage, not all six. Or if the disadvantage was introduced in 2NC, go for links or impacts, but not both.

2. *Counterplans.* Again, go for a set of 2AC responses. Go for topicality, competitiveness, or disadvantages. The affirmative has the luxury of picking and choosing which counterplan answers that eliminate the counterplan to extend.

3. *Case attacks.* You don't have to win every piece of evidence and every argument on case, but you need to win enough to outweigh the disadvantage risks. You need to win enough of the prima facie burdens of the 1AC. If you have more than one advantage, you may choose to jettison the weakest one.

Tips

- *Be concise.* Use abbreviations when you speak, such as "T" for topicality and "DA" for disadvantage. This is a very common time-saving technique. Highlight your evidence, coloring only the sentences that prove what you need, and then just read those passages. Eliminate pet phrases such as "you know," "like," and "what we are arguing here is," as they merely waste your time and do not add argumentative force to your presentation. You have a lot to do and not much time to do it in. Try to improve your "word economy," just as you would in an essay with a limited number of words assigned but a fairly broad topic. Don't over-explain. Prepare your notes completely before your speech. Place important words first on the argument title (label).

- *Refer to previous evidence.* You can't read much evidence in the 1AR. Extend the evidence from the 1AC and 2AC. Read additional evidence where it is needed most.

- *Be organized.* Organization is critical for the 1AR. Have all your materials in order before you begin to speak.

- *Order issues.* Always put topicality first, then go to disadvantages and counterplans. Go to case last. Ending on familiar ground helps you allocate the time better.

- *Allocate your time.* Count the number of issues you will be covering just before you deliver your speech so you know how much time you can spend on each argument. Have your partner help you keep track of time.

- *Exploit negative contradictions.* Look for some of these common contradictions:
  - *Inherency-Disadvantage.* If the negative says that the status quo is working, then why haven't the disadvantages happened?
  - *Solvency-Disadvantage.* You may be able to grant a negative solvency argument in order to evade the link to a disadvantage.
  - *Disadvantage-Disadvantage.* Negatives often run disadvantages with contradictory theses. You can grant one disadvantage to prevent another. Caution: don't grant negative arguments that could beat you. For example, if you are going to grant one solvency argument to evade a disadvantage, make sure you have another solvency mechanism left to gain an advantage.

Always give the 1AR a high-five after she speaks. It looks good to the judge.

Second Negative Rebuttal (2NR)

Now is the time to focus the debate even more. The negative search for truth ends in the 2NR. Winning requires the 2NR to choose the issues and approach to create a persuasive bottom line for the negative. The 2NR cannot pursue everything in the debate, because the judge must be told which arguments to consider. If not given a rationale or "bottom line" position, the judge will not know why to vote negative. A winning 2NR writes the ballot for the judge.

There are two ways to win in the 2NR: Win the Drop or Win the Position.

Win the Drop. Many debates are decided because the 1AR could not cover the issues from the 2NC and 1NR or because debaters could not flow well and missed responses. The 2NR's job is to emphasize the dropped argument and explain why it is sufficient to vote negative. This entails weighing the dropped argument against the affirmative case. Examples include dropped disadvantages, topicality, or major case arguments.

Win the Position. The 2NR must pull all negative issues together in a way that jettisons all irrelevant material and focuses the debate on a single negative strategy. Remember the importance of narrowing the debate to a simple bottom line position.

Regardless of which tactic you use, you will still need to win specific kinds of arguments in order to win the round. Here are some examples:

High Impact Disadvantages. Win a disadvantage with an impact that outweighs the case advantages(s).

Topicality. Argue that topicality is the absolute voting issue. In other words, the judge should decide topicality before evaluating the rest of the debate. You may combine the topicality issue with some other issue or you may wish to pursue topicality exclusively. Most judges would prefer that if you plan to win the debate on topicality, you spend the entire 2NR on that issue, because if you win it, you win the debate.

Prima Facie Issue. You may beat the affirmative on its own ground by defeating one of the required stock issues in its case, such as significance, inherency, or solvency. The only problem with using this approach is that without a good disadvantage or critique, the affirmative can always argue that the judge has nothing to lose by voting affirmative since, at worst, nothing bad will happen and we might as well try to improve the status quo. This is why it is important to make arguments that turn the case, arguments charging that the plan will make the problems identified by the case worse.

The Counterplan Position. You may focus exclusively on the counterplan position, especially if it competes with the affirmative's plan and the negative's disadvantages are unique to the affirmative plan. If you have a better way to deal with the problem (counterplan solvency) that avoids other problems created by the affirmative plan (net benefits to the counterplan) and you show that the counterplan is competitive (we cannot do both the affirmative plan and the counterplan but must choose), then just the counterplan may win the debate for you.

The Counterplan + Disadvantage Position. Have a counterplan that gains the affirmative advantage while avoiding your disadvantage. This is a very effective strategy.

Deciding which issues to focus on can be difficult, but you must focus. **If you do not choose, you will lose!**

Tips

- *Try these phrases to preempt the 2AR.*
    "No new arguments in the 2AR."
    "No new cross-applications in the 2AR."
    "If you can't trace it back to the 1AR, ignore it."
- *Don't "go for everything."* Now is the time to focus on your best issues.
- *Extend your negative arguments from the 2NC and 1NR.* Don't just summarize. There are two parts to extending an argument: denying the truth or relevance of the opposition argument *and* explaining why yours is better. Many 2NRs fall into the "no clash trap." You must draw the connection between your arguments and your opponent's. Try these phrases:
    "They have good evidence here, but ours answers it."
    "Our uniqueness evidence is much more recent."
    "On topicality, they do not extend their own definition; our definition is the only one in the debate."

Each of these phrases considers the opponent's argument and attempts to answer it.

- *Present your best arguments first.* Spend a significant amount of time presenting the argument on which you want the judge to vote.
- *Compare arguments.* Frequently, debaters assume that if they extend their arguments, the judge will simply know that their arguments are more important than their opponents'. Do not be so trusting. Use these phrases:

  "They may be winning a little advantage, but the disadvantage will outweigh."

  "They have a good definition, but it unfairly expands the grounds of the topic, so it is not good for debate."

  "Even if they are winning a risk of a turn on this disadvantage, the counterplan will solve the turn."
- *Take all of your preparation time.* Use all of your prep time to write out responses to the issues you want to discuss. Take a moment to look over the flow and be certain you are not missing an important affirmative response. Ask your partner what issues he or she might think important.

Second Affirmative Rebuttal (2AR)

The affirmative gets the last speech in the debate, and it needs to take full advantage. The general strategy of the 2AR is to re-establish case advantage(s) and to minimize or take out the impacts of the negative arguments. In order to minimize the impact of the negative arguments, don't address negative arguments in the order they were presented—set your own agenda, first presenting what you think is the most compelling reason to vote affirmative. This trick tends to de-emphasize the arguments that the 2NR claimed were critical in the debate.

Tips

- *Extend.* Don't just repeat or summarize your arguments.

- *Address only the strongest 1AR responses.* You do not need all of them; just use the best of them.
- *Sequence.* Set your own agenda. Deal with the 2NR's issues comprehensively, but focus on your own issues. End with a short explanation of why you have won the round.
- *Retell the story.* Every affirmative has a narrative behind it, a story about the faults of the status quo and how there will be a happy ending if the plan is adopted. Likewise, the negative tells a different story, that things are not so bad now, that the plan will fail, and that the future with the plan will be very bleak. Emphasize how your story is more plausible or more compelling than the negative's.
- *Allocate time the same as the 2NR.* Spend time on the issues that the 2NR focused on. It will do no good to spend 3 minutes re-explaining the case if the 2NR spent 4 minutes on a disadvantage, a counterplan, and a topicality violation.
- *Wrap up the debate.* Explain why you should still win the round even if you have lost a few issues. If you are unable to beat an argument, then say something like this: "Even if you grant the negative a partial solvency argument, then you should still vote affirmative on the chance the plan will solve . . ." Or, "Even with only 50% solvency, you should still vote affirmative since it is comparatively better than the status quo."

Remember: the 2NR and the 2AR represent each team's final opportunity to explain its point of view to the judge. If you have anything important to say, now is the time to say it! Arguing with the judge after the round is over might make you feel better, but it won't change the outcome of the debate and it will probably make the judge dislike you.

Timeline for a Policy Debate

Time is one of the most precious things in any debate. If you use your time properly, you will be far more likely to win. The timeline below will show you what each debater should be doing before the round and during each speech. Don't be afraid to refer to it in your practice debates or during your first few tournaments. After a while you will routinely use time in roughly this fashion.

- *Learn about judges.* Find out what arguments they like, what arguments they do not like, and what their stylistic preferences are.
- *Learn about your opponents.* Find out what their strengths are and what their weaknesses are.
- *Learn what your opponents argued the last time they debated on that side of the topic.* Always save the postings from previous debates so you can ask a team they debated before.
- *Develop a strategy based on this information.*
- *Consult with your coach.*
- *Capture the table by getting to the room first.* Most classrooms have only one good table. You will be able to organize your materials more effectively if you have it.
- *Make sure everyone is ready.* Do not delay the start of the debate once the judge is in position.

DURING THE DEBATE

First Affirmative Constructive Speech (1AC)—presents prepared speech of the affirmative case

    1A: SPEAKING

    2A: Prepare materials and anticipate arguments.

    1N: Flow, develop strategy based on case, construct case arguments.

    2N: Flow, assist 1N, think of questions for cross-examination.

Second Negative Cross-Examines First Affirmative (2N cx 1A)

1A: Answer questions using 1AC speech. Be cautious, explain case, and provide definitions.

2A: Listen for errors in answers, anticipate negative arguments.

1N: Prepare to speak.

2N: Question 1A, ask questions that help partner, get a solid explanation of opposition plan.

Preparation Time

1A: Consult with partner and anticipate answers.

2A: Same.

1N: Prepare to speak. Use no more than 10% of prep time.

2N: Assist partner.

First Negative Constructive Speech (1NC)—presents off-case arguments and attacks the case.

1A: Flow with detail, watch for contradictions and evidence. Assist 2A as requested. Think of questions for cross-examination.

2A: Listen, flow, and prepare to speak. If you need help (for example, finding something), have 1A do that while you continue listening and flowing.

1N: SPEAKING

2N: Listen, flow, choose an argument, and prepare to extend it.

First Affirmative Cross-Examines First Negative (1A cx 1N)

1A: Ask questions for 2AC (topicality, link, competition, relevance).

2A: Prepare to speak.

1N: Answer questions based on your arguments, avoid other topics.

2N: Listen to answers for errors and prepare to extend an argument. Prepare for your speech.

Preparation Time

1A: Assist 2A in preparation.

2A: Prepare to speak. Use no more than 25% of prep time.

1N: Discuss which issues to go for in the 2NC/1NR block. Decide on preliminary division of labor.

2N: Same.

Second Affirmative Constructive Speech (2AC)—Answers or turns everything 1N said and extends the case. Establishes the framework for the judge to use in making the decision in the affirmative's favor.

1A: Listen and flow carefully, make sure to note precise answers to arguments to help 2A's flow. 2A may think of answers while speaking, and you will need to help her fill these in on her flow after the speech.

2A: SPEAKING

1N: Flow carefully, paying special attention to issues to be extended in 1NR. Think of questions for cross-examination; help 2N.

2N: Prepare to speak. If you need something, have the 1N look for it when the argument she will extend in 1NR is not being discussed.

First Negative Cross-Examines Second Affirmative (1N cx 2A)

1A: Listen for problems.

2A: Answer questions fully, don't evade. Explain, when possible, why you think your issues are more important than the negative's.

1N: Ask questions for 2N, explore answers as a possible way to kick out of negative issues you may wish to discard.

2N: Prepare to speak.

Preparation Time

1A: Review 2AC answers and add new ones to the flow. Consider which 2AC answers to extend in 1AR.

2A: Same.

1N: Assist 2N in preparation.

2N: Prepare to speak. Use no more than 40% of prep time.

Second Negative Constructive Speech (2NC)—Kicks out of negative issues it wishes to discard. Begins weighing process to explain why the negative issues outweigh the affirmative's case.

    1A: Prepare to speak; ask 2A for help if necessary.

    2A: Flow carefully to determine which 2AC answers to address; think of questions for cross-examination.

    1N: Listen to 2NC so that you can be consistent with your partner; prepare to speak.

    2N: SPEAKING

Second Affirmative Cross-Examines Second Negative (2A cx 2N)

    1A: Prepare to speak. Use this valuable preparation time.

    2A: Ask questions with focus to clarify issues.

    1N: Prepare to speak but continue to listen.

    2N: Answer questions fully, emphasize the superiority of arguments and evidence.

First Negative Rebuttal (1NR)—Concentrates on one or more issues and wins them decisively. Indicates weighing process to explain why the issues she is dealing with outweigh the affirmative case.

    1A: Flow; prepare to speak.

    2A: Flow carefully; help 1A as necessary.

    1N: SPEAKING

    2N: Flow carefully and determine how to extend your arguments. Put a star next to the most important issues and arguments.

Preparation Time

    1A: Prepare to speak. Use no more than 50% of prep time.

    2A: Assist 1A.

    1N: Listen to 2N review 1NR arguments. Give feedback.

    2N: Quietly repeat the 1NR arguments to 1N. Practice saying what 1NR just said and you will give a better 2NR when dealing with those issues. The 1N should indicate openly which arguments from the 1NR are the strongest.

First Affirmative Rebuttal (1AR)—Answers all the issues in the negative block but focuses on certain 2AC responses (turns, dropped answers, stronger answers, etc.).

- 1A: SPEAKING
- 2A: Listen and flow carefully, watch time allocation, signal the 1AR on time.
- 1N: Listen and flow carefully. Watch for strategic errors and openings.
- 2N: Listen and flow; prepare to speak.

Preparation Time

- 1A: Review 1AR and consider opportunities. Look at round strategically.
- 2A: Review 1AR on most troubling issue; consider which answers are best. Now is the time to have a discussion during 2NR preparation time.
- 1N: Assist and advise partner.
- 2N: Use all remaining negative prep time. Compare the affirmative and negative policy plans, discuss options, *then* prep. Get the broad perspective of your speech down first, and then work on specifics.

Second Negative Rebuttal (2NR)—Focuses on critical negative issues, minimizes the affirmative case, weighs the round for the judge using ideas begun in 2NC.

- 1A: Flow; look for opportunities and errors.
- 2A: Flow; prepare to speak.
- 1N: Flow; watch for suggestions to make later.
- 2N: SPEAKING

Preparation Time

    1A: Assist 2A.

    2A: Prepare to speak. Use all remaining affirmative prep time.

    1N: Kick back. Look confident.

    2N: Kick back. Look confident.

Second Affirmative Rebuttal (2AR)—Counters remaining negative issues, defends case, engages in weighing, and shows the judge how the affirmative's policy plan is better than the status quo or the counterplan.

    1A: Flow for comments and advice for next time.

    2A: SPEAKING

    1N: Flow for comments; note any tricks your opponent played so that you can anticipate them the next time your debate this team.

    2N: Same.

AFTER THE ROUND

- Save flowsheets and label completely, indicating tournament, round, side, opponent, and judge.
- Shake hands with opponents.
- Make sure you have all your materials.
- Don't leave the room until the judge determines the winner.
- Receive any comments from the judge.
- Be inquisitive of the judge but not rude.
- Take notes on what the judge says so you can debate better in front of her in the future.

Part Three

Debaters Have Skills

Debating takes skills and real debaters have them. They are skills that will serve you well throughout your life. It isn't enough to know the structure and the theory of policy debate, as the debating itself requires that you show a number of complex behaviors that can be challenging to learn and develop.

This chapter covers most of the basic skills that you will need to debate successfully. Skills are a special part of learning. To develop skills you need practice. Just as you do when learning a sport, in the intellectual game of debate you need to sharpen your skills through practice and feedback.

Speaking

It all starts with your voice and your ability to communicate orally with the judge and the other team. Your delivery is extremely important, for without good delivery your audience will not pay attention to your ideas or their understanding of what you are saying will be limited. Your public speaking ability is central to your performance as a debater.

You will need to be flexible in your style of delivery. Some judges like the faster, more intense delivery that is found in so many policy debates, while others prefer a slower and more relaxed style. Of course, there are countless judges in between. We will pursue this later, in Chapter 18 on adapting to judges, but for now realize that one style may well not fit all, but the ideas contained in this section should apply to the vast majority of judges no matter what speed you speak at.

Remember that when there is a contradiction between what you are saying and the way you are saying it, people will usually focus on the way you are saying something. You may claim you are calm, but if you sound upset that is what the audience believes. You may be nervous, but if you seem calm and in control the audience is likely to believe that you are.

Goals

Listeners will form an overall impression of you from the way you speak. Prepare yourself to make a good impression by working toward the following goals:

1. Be clear and comprehensible: the judge needs to understand what you say.
2. Be credible: good delivery makes the judge want to believe you.
3. Be memorable: you want the judge to remember what you said and note it.

THE DYNAMIC SPEAKER

People tend to listen to and believe dynamic speakers. You are a dynamic speaker when you speak with energy, enthusiasm, commitment, and variety. You are not dynamic when you appear indifferent, lack confidence, speak in a monotone, or are just plain boring. Act like you care about the arguments and about winning this debate.

The dynamic speaker does not always sound loud and forceful but punctuates her speech with some softness and some sympathetic tones. Your quiet and calm moments make your louder and more excited moments more powerful. People can be easily distracted while you are speaking. A dynamic style that involves changes and variety helps the audience remain focused on your ideas. A dynamic speaking style will also help your audience accept what you are saying, because you sound like you believe what you are saying.

Being a dynamic speaker is not as easy as just talking loudly or trying to look more confident. You need to balance a variety of factors in order to deliver a really dynamic speech. Three factors create dynamism:

1. *Variation.* Never repeat the same hand gesture or voice tone. It causes people to lose focus. You become boring, and people's attention drifts. Mix it up.
2. *Emphasis.* Use your delivery (voice, gestures, etc.) to emphasize and highlight the important arguments and the important words in your evidence. People will not remember everything you say, even if they

are taking notes. However, if you emphasize important phrases and sentences, they are likely to retain this information.

3. *Naturalness*. Variation is important, but too much variation seems unnatural. Stay within your natural range of speaking (voice, gestures, body language, etc.). Be yourself, because if the judge thinks you are trying to be someone you are not, she will not believe you. Impress her with your dynamism and arguments.

Applying Dynamism Factors to Delivery

Many people are afraid of public speaking because they have little experience in doing it. But if you understand how to use your voice, gestures, and body, you will be more comfortable and find the experience far more pleasant than you thought. You will be a more interesting and dynamic speaker and you will better hold the audience's attention.

VOICE

The human voice is the most important communication mechanism that human beings have. You know that you can often tell what friends are thinking by the way they speak. A tone of voice can communicate concern, joy, fear, or curiosity. Below are the basic elements of the voice that you can manipulate to enhance your communication.

Volume: Change volume for emphasis but don't talk too loudly or too softly. You can emphasize by being softer as well as louder, especially if the point you are making is more emotional and you pause slightly before using a softer voice for emphasis. Before your debate, assess the acoustic space in which you will be speaking. Make sure your softest voice can be heard by the farthest listener and that your loudest voice will not irritate your closest listener.

Pitch: Change your pitch for emphasis but don't speak in a tone that is unusual or out of character. Your pitch indicates your emotional state.

A high-pitched voice indicates excitement or perhaps anger, while a low-pitched voice indicates composure. Raise your pitch slightly when you want to appear excited and concerned; lower it when you want to appear calm and in control.

Speed: Speed also helps you emphasize key points. Slow down for important material, such as a crucial distinction. But remember not to speak too slow or too fast. If you are too slow you will not have time to present all your arguments; if you are too fast, the audience may not be able to understand what you are saying. In any case, always speaking at the same speed is boring.

FACE

Your face is the most expressive part of your body. Studies show that people pay close attention to facial expressions, so use expressions that match your points. Don't send mixed signals. If you are sad about the content of your argument ("Thousands of children die of starvation"), don't smile.

EYE CONTACT

Many people associate eye contact with honesty, so remember to make eye contact with the judge and the audience. Eye contact also personalizes your presentation, making it appear more like a conversation than a formal communication event. Don't stare at audience members, but a brief moment of eye contact can be a very powerful stylistic element.

BODY MOVEMENT

When you speak, your present yourself as a whole being who has something important to say. Consequently, your body movements are extremely important. Follow these three rules to aid your presentation.

1. *Vary your movements.* Repeating movements such as rocking back and forth or pacing make you look a little odd and somewhat uncomfortable. More natural movements, such as slightly turning from

one side to the other occasionally, are welcome and make you look comfortable.

2. *Face the audience.* An open body posture makes you look more involved and relaxed. Stand up straight and engage the audience directly, instead of leaning over and looking down.

3. *Use your body movement for emphasis.* You might lean toward the audience to make an important point or step toward your opponents ever so slightly to indicate that you disagree with something they have said. Don't be afraid to move around a bit, but don't stray too far from your flowsheet and your evidence. Your movements should always be slow and deliberate to indicate you are calm and self-assured.

GESTURES

Using your hands to help express what you are saying is a natural human trait. But because we feel uncomfortable, we often don't use natural gestures when speaking before an audience. The audience finds this odd, so remember to use your natural gestures. But also remember that you will need to make sure your gestures are visible to the audience. Bring your gestures out in front of you and to the side so that people can see them and you look more dynamic. Apply three rules to your gestures.

1. *Vary them.* Repeating the same gesture can seem mechanical and boring.

2. *Use gestures to emphasize the important ideas in your speech.*

3. *Make sure that your gestures are not distracting.* Always avoid touching yourself, playing with a pen or things in your pockets, or making unusual gestures that may seem odd to the audience.

The Physical Elements of Speech

We speak through a natural physical system that we use to get our points across. You will use this complex system every time you debate. Your debate speaking will improve if you are aware of how it operates. It is useful to understand that your body contains several mechanisms that work together to produce speech. It does not just come from your head or your throat, but from a complex interactive system. Awareness of this system can help you find problems and eliminate them.

PARTS OF YOUR SPEECH SYSTEM

Diaphragm: this is the energy source of your speaking mechanism. Too often debaters bend over while speaking and thus cannot use the diaphragm properly to power their speaking system. Try this experiment. Stand up and locate your diaphragm at the base of the rib cage; bend over and read aloud for as long as you can without inhaling. Do the same while standing straight and see if you can speak longer.

Trachea (windpipe): this conveys air to and from the lungs. If you breathe improperly you can hear the air rasping through your trachea.

Larynx (voice box): this is where the vibrations take place that are your voice. Locate your Adam's apple; this is the cartilage that surrounds your larynx.

Soft palate: this determines nasal qualities. Stand and hold your nose. Then say the vowels (a, e, i, o, u). Try the same thing with your nose open. Repeat the exercise with the consonants m, n, and ng. This exercise will help you become aware of how your soft palate influences your speaking.

Mouth: this is where articulation comes from. Try to talk first with a pen in your mouth, then without opening your mouth very wide and keeping your teeth together, and finally with your mouth moving as needed to articulate. See how much better you sound when you really use your mouth.

CARING FOR YOUR SPEECH SYSTEM

To be an effective speaker you need to take care of your speech system and avoid activities that can damage or limit its effectiveness. Here are some basic guidelines:

1. *Don't smoke.* Not only is it bad for your health, but it can also reduce your clarity as a speaker and slow you down. Smoking inhibits breathing, which is important in using your voice during a debate.
2. *Always stand when you speak.* Don't crush your diaphragm.
3. *Breathe properly.* Don't bend over and read. Breathe only at the end of a sentence.
4. In the days before a tournament, *"wake up" your vocal chords and "oil" your larynx daily* by reading the newspaper out loud and fast while overemphasizing pronunciation.
5. *Don't take your pen with you when you speak.* If you do, keep it out of your mouth.
6. *Avoid dairy products.* Milk and other dairy products coat the vocal cords, preventing you from talking at maximum speed and causing stumbles and vocal slips. Some people have similar problems if they drink liquids with too much sugar. Drink water, diet soft drinks, and iced tea during a tournament.

Giving a Good First Impression

First impressions are important. As soon as you walk into the debate room and the judge sees you, the "show" of the debate has begun. Whenever you are within the sight of your judge, consciously or unconsciously, she will be evaluating you. Remember that you will want to seem:

- *Competitive.* Express a serious demeanor and be ready to debate on time.
- *Confident.* Convey that you feel good about what you are saying.
- *Courteous.* Be friendly and mature but don't flatter. And certainly don't be rude.
- *Credible.* Show credibility by being dynamic. Dynamism has been shown to increase perceived credibility of speakers.
- *Commanding.* Dress appropriately. Don't use street language or swear.

Speaking Drills*

Your speaking skills are like any other skills—you need to practice and refine them if you want to maintain and extend them. And you need to correct any problems you have. Below is a list of some drills you can use to address common problems. Conduct regular drills with your teammates. Make contests out of them—and have fun!

BREATHING PROBLEMS

Common problems include not taking enough breaths (running out of air at the end of a sentence or the end of a piece of evidence) and breathing incorrectly (taking huge gasps of air—actually a symptom of not taking enough breaths).

Failure to breathe at natural pause points in the evidence. Take a small breath at each punctuation mark—commas, periods, semi-colons, colons, etc.

Failure to breathe at natural pause points in the speech. Say the argument title, take a breath, read the citation, take a breath, read the evidence itself (breathing at punctuation marks), then repeat the process with other pieces of evidence.

Failure to breathe from the diaphragm. Hold a light chair chest high in front of you, with your arms as straight as possible. Read a piece of evidence that is lying on the seat of the chair. You should be breathing from the diaphragm during this process. Now put down the chair and re-read the evidence normally. You will likely be breathing from your throat. Repeat the exercise until you can feel the difference and can breathe from the diaphragm while reading normally.

ENUNCIATION PROBLEMS

Unless you clearly enunciate your words, listeners will tire of the extra work they have to do to understand you. Clear enunciation will

---

*This material is adapted from a lecture I gave on speaking drills delivered at the World Debate Institute at the University of Vermont.

assist you in keeping your listeners' attention and will improve their comprehension.

- Read a piece of evidence slowly, hitting all of the hard consonants (b, d, g, k, p, t, etc.) and enunciating each and every syllable. Gradually increase your speed while you continue to over-enunciate and hit all of the hard consonants.
- Read evidence while you have a pen in your mouth. You will over-articulate, which is a good thing.
- Read tongue twisters at high speed.

PITCH PROBLEMS

Often the pitch of your voice will go much higher than your normal pitch when you talk fast. Pitch problems are another symptom of improper breathing, so use the same chair drill that you use for breathing problems to work to correct this.

MONOTONE OR SINGSONG DELIVERY

Sometimes you focus so much on the content of your speech and watching your time allocation that you fall into bad speech patterns, such as utilizing the same pattern for each sentence (singsong delivery) or using a single vocal pattern that becomes boring (monotone delivery). Here are two ways you can deal with these problems.

- Mark the words that require emphasis in a brief. Now read the brief, altering your emphasis when you get to those words. Emphasizing words by speaking them just a little louder can be a more effective way to highlight important words.
- Read a piece of evidence or brief slowly, and in your normal mode of speaking (like it was a conversation rather than reading evidence). Hints of your personality should come through. Now build up the speed, maintaining that personality influence along the way.

While you want to have variation in the way you deliver your speech, you can go too far in one direction. This can be true of the volume at which you speak. You need to be neither too quiet nor too loud. These exercises can help if you need to work on these issues.

Too quiet
- Practice reading at the top of your voice. Of course, you would not do this in a debate, but it is a good way to learn to increase your volume.

Too loud
Generally caused by improper breathing. Thus, use the drills above, or
- Practice reading at a whisper.

OTHER DELIVERY PROBLEMS

Here are some other common delivery problems and drills to help you overcome them.

Mush Mouth—articulation is unclear
- Abade drill—you should say abade (ah baa dee) over and over and over, steadily increasing speed, and continuing to have clean and clear breaks between the syllables.
- Open the mouth—you should open your mouth to an exaggerated degree when you read something at a conversational rate (you will think this is silly looking and that it feels silly). Now do the same at a faster rate of delivery—when people are flowing and judging, they won't notice the exaggerated articulation effort.

Choppy Speech—lots of unnatural or unnecessary pauses and stumbles
- Get a rhythm—try to learn a natural rhythm that will keep you at a constant speed. One technique is to read to music that has a clear and constant beat, or have someone clap your hands or tap a pen on the desk while you are talking, slowly increasing the beat as you progress through the speech.

- Read ahead—you should practice reading a couple of words ahead of where your mouth is. Often stumbles and pauses are caused by suddenly encountering new or unexpected words. Thus, if you see the words a partial second before you speak them, fewer pauses will result.
- Ignore stuttering and stumbles—a lot of debaters will "back up" and try to correctly pronounce a word, or will try to stop a stutter and correctly say a word. That gets them out of their rhythm, forces them to almost stop speaking for a second, and then re-start again. Instead, you should try to just keep going when you make an error (at a fast rate of speaking, few judges will notice if someone mispronounces a word or two)—it's like a record that is stuck in the same groove—hit the arm and get it to a new groove; don't stop the record and merely start over at the same place.

OTHER DRILLS TO IMPROVE SPEAKING

You will never be such a good speaker that practice cannot help you. Even if you have no serious speaking issues to work through, you should keep practicing your delivery. Here are some exercises that you should consider using regularly.

- *Get in the habit of reading through your briefs before you file them.* The more familiar you are with their evidence, the more fluid your speaking should be.
- *Hold technique drills using material that you have no interest in using in a debate.* For example, read Plato or Aristotle at warp drive, or read the classified page of the newspaper. You will then focus on your speaking technique rather than on the specific content of the material.
- *Practice building up speed gradually as you deliver your speech.* Begin every speech relatively slowly and then work up to normal speed. This way you will tend not to overshoot your capabilities. A lot of times you may start at a faster rate than you can maintain over the course of a speech. Building up to your maximum rate means you are more likely to maintain a sustainable rate. Gradually working up to speed

also allows the judge and your opponents a few seconds to get used to your particular speaking style before a critical piece of evidence or argument comes flying by.

- *Give a practice speech, and immediately stop whenever a problem occurs, then start over from the beginning.* You will quickly tire of doing this and work to improve your delivery.
- *Videotape yourself debating.* That way you not only hear your annoying habits, you see them as well.
- *Practice, practice, practice.* Get into the habit of practicing at least 5–10 minutes every day. Have practice sessions giving speeches without evidence as well as reading evidence.

Drills are for *everyone*. Novices need them to get used to speaking in the debate situation. Experienced debaters need them to cure bad habits. Even award-winning debaters need them to maintain their skills and move up on the speaker award list.

10

Flowing

Taking notes ("flow sheeting" or "flowing" are the debate terms) properly is an essential skill for debaters at all levels. In fact, next to speaking, it is the most important skill you will need for winning. You must write down your opponent's arguments so that you can remember them and respond to them in order. Until you learn to take notes properly, many of the ideas and arguments in the debate may pass you by. Learn to take notes early in your debate involvement and keep working on perfecting your skills throughout your debate career.

The Basics

You may have learned how to take notes for your classes, but that will not be sufficient for the rigors of debating. You will need to start over again in learning the system for taking notes that all debaters use.

MATERIALS

This may seem simplistic, but the materials you use are important in flowing. Use a pen that moves smoothly over the paper and allows you to write quickly. Write in black, and use ink that does not smear. Try a medium point pen, though if you write small use a fine point, and if you write large you can get away with a broad point pen. Make sure your pen is comfortable in your hand, and always have lots of the right kinds of pens available.

Most debaters flow on yellow legal pads. Yellow because it is easy to read (especially with black ink!), and legal size (8.5" x 14") because it has more space. Some debaters buy a ream of white legal size paper because it is more economical. Don't do this. Use pads rather than individual sheets so that you can easily keep multiple pages attached.

ORGANIZING THE FLOWSHEETS

Debaters' notes are organized into separate flows for each major issue, so you will use multiple pages, each of which you will divide vertically into 7 columns. As you have learned, policy debate calls for eight speeches, but you need only seven columns on each flowsheet page because the 2NC-1NR speeches occur one right after the other and so share a column. The seven columns you will need are 1AC, 1NC, 2AC, 2NC-1NR, 1AR, 2NR, 2AR. Draw these columns on your pages well before the debate starts. As a speech is given, write down what is being said in that speech's column. If, for example, it is an argument against the case made in 1NC, you would flow it on the case pad, in the 1NC column, next to the part of the case the argument clashes with. You should flow the entire debate, even after you have given your speech, so that you can help your partner.

When organizing your flowsheets, remember to:

1. *Use separate note pads.* It is often useful to have several different pads and put different kinds of arguments on each one. For example, the affirmative case could be on one pad, the negative topicality and pro-cedural arguments could be on another, the negative disadvantages could be on a third pad, and the negative counterplan could be on a fourth pad, depending on whether these issues make an appearance at all. This use of separate pads allows you to keep your notes organized around major types of issues in the debate. You don't want a bunch of loose sheets of paper flying all over.

2. *Leave room on your flow.* Don't crowd arguments together. If arguments are all packed together on your flowsheet, it will be hard to refer to it

and read from it when you are speaking. Do not be afraid to use many pages, with a different major point on each page. Also, leave space between issues as they are introduced. You may need that space later.

USING SYMBOLIC VOCABULARY

People speak more quickly than you can write, so use symbols to stand for concepts. Below are symbols we commonly encounter in an argumentative situation.

Logic symbols

↑   increasing or increases
↓   decreasing or decreases
=   is or the same as
→   causes or leads to
>   greater than
<   less than

You can negate these symbols by drawing a line through them. Thus, you get:

↑̸   not increasing
↓̸   not decreasing
≠   not lead to or not cause

Debate symbols

×   piece of evidence used by speaker
?   no answer to this
Δ   change
∅   assertion that should have been proved
⊗   evidence does not prove argument claimed

You also will use abbreviations for common debate terms such as these:

AC = affirmative case

AP = affirmative plan

CP = counterplan

DA = disadvantage

H = harm

K = critique

SV = solvency

T = topicality

VI = voting issue

Use abbreviations for common terms in the topic as well. You will have to develop these on your own. If you are making an abbreviation for the first time, try leaving the vowels out; thus, "hospital" becomes "hsptl." As you become more familiar with an abbreviation, you can drop out more and more characters to increase efficiency.

The example below shows how you would use symbols and abbreviations for a simple argument.

> "Legislating new mandatory minimum sentences would let criminals know that they will do time if they get caught, and so they will think twice about committing more crimes."

becomes:

$$\uparrow MM \rightarrow \text{percep of crims} = \downarrow Cr$$

When you combine argument and debate symbols with debate and topic abbreviations, you are able to quickly write down what your opponent's arguments mean in a way that makes sense to you and that you can interpret to the judge.

Flowing Speech by Speech

Not every speech and every speaker uses the same techniques for flowsheeting. Just as different speeches have different obligations, different speakers need to flowsheet the debate in slightly different ways.

First Affirmative Constructive (1AC). Everyone flows this speech. The affirmative team members should preflow this speech on Post-it® notes or legal pads so that they can detail what they will say without having to do it over again before every debate. Use lots of space between each argument.

First Negative Constructive (1NC). Everyone flows this speech. The negative may have its generic arguments already preflowed because they may have received an outline of the affirmative case before the debate through scouting or disclosure. During the cross-examination period that follows this speech, the 2NC flows onto the 1NC's flowsheet any responses that the 1NC didn't get to write out.

Second Affirmative Constructive (2AC). Everyone flows this speech. Use cross-examination to get parts that you missed or have your partner fill in the missing information.

Second Negative Constructive (2NC). Everyone but the 1NC flows this speech. The 1NR listens but primarily is preparing to give the 1NR.

First Negative Rebuttal (1NR). Everyone flows this speech.

First Affirmative Rebuttal (1AR). Everyone flows this speech.

Second Negative Rebuttal (2NR). Everyone flows this speech.

Second Affirmative Rebuttal (2AR). Everyone flows this speech.

Helpful Tips for Flowing

Because flowing is vital to winning a debate, here are some guidelines you should consider.

1. *Use your opponent's structure if he has one.* Structure and label all the arguments on your flow the same way that the speaker you are flowing does. Be sure to write down all the numbers and letters you hear on your flow so that you can refer to specific subpoints later in the debate.

2. *Don't be disorganized.* When flowing the disorganized speaker, do not follow his example. Write all of his arguments in one column on a separate legal pad. Then in your speech, answer all of his arguments in the order they were presented. Then go back to *your original* structure and point out what you are winning and what your opponent failed to answer in his speech.

3. *Use preflows.* Flow all of your prepared arguments clearly before you speak. Sometimes you can preflow your arguments on Post-it® notes and just stick them on your flow when the time comes to use them.

4. *Use your partner.* If you can't flow all of your own arguments before you speak, hand your flow to your partner during cross-examination and have her fill in your flow for you. Use the other team's prep time to talk to your partner about arguments you might have missed.

5. *Label your arguments on your briefs and preflows.* Use accurate, precise, and specific labels no more than four words long. Put the crucial words first. If you label arguments correctly, you will be able to give a better speech because your judge, partners, and opponents will find you easier to flow.

6. *Write down everything you can.* Focus all your attention and energy on this task.

7. *Never give up.* If you miss something, get the next argument. Once you stop flowing, you are opting out of meaningful participation in the debate.

8. *Ask to see the flows of your coaches and fellow debaters.* Learn from them.

9. *Practice!* Watch a debate and flow it as best you can. This can be especially useful if you flow elimination round debate after you have been eliminated. You will be able to focus just on flowing without being distracted by participating in the debate.

11

Organizing Arguments

Poor organization can sabotage excellent ideas. Likewise, proper organization can enhance average ideas and contribute to your success. This is more true in debate than in other communication situations. Certainly the content of your arguments is important, but judges also evaluate how you organize your ideas.

As a debater, one of your most important goals is to present material in a logical manner and relate ideas in meaningful ways so that the judge can easily connect your responses to the arguments they are answering. Unless your ideas work well together and unless the judge can connect your ideas to those of your opponent, you will have difficulty winning the debate.

Learn to Build an Outline

When you build arguments and advocacy positions in a debate, you need to remember basic outlining techniques:

- *Use proper notation.* Outlines (and debate arguments) have letter and number alternations so that one level of substructure can be differentiated from another. Major points are often expressed with roman numerals (I, II, III, IV, etc.), subtopics of major points are letters (A, B, C, D, etc.), and particulars about subtopics are numbers (1, 2, 3, etc.).

You need two ideas to begin a subdivision of any point, or else the single subdivision would be the more general point. In other words, you need a B to justify an A, and a 2 to justify a 1. Here is an example:

I. Major point that you are making
   A. Subtopic in support of I
   B. Another subtopic in support of I
      1. Specific point about B
      2. Another specific point about B
II. Another major point you are making
   A. Subtopic in support of II
   B. Another subtopic in support of II

- *Organize based on major points.* Organize your ideas under major headings. These major headings might represent major argumentative burdens, such as stock issues, or else be based on separate advantages of your affirmative plan. Make sure that the major points are distinct from one another. If an idea is vital to your conclusion, include it as a major point. Put major points in the proper chronological order: causes before effects, background before conclusions, etc.

- *3. Use proper subordination.* Arrange specific points under the major ideas they support. Some of these points will naturally group together into further subgroups. For example, you may claim that your plan will enhance individual rights (a major idea) and then under that you might list groups that will have additional rights, such as business people, travelers, etc. This organization of ideas is essential to debate success and to becoming a critical thinker. Ideas can be sorted by distinct concepts, general or specific nature, different steps in a logical process, etc. For example, in constructing a disadvantage you might have subordination such as the following:

   A. The affirmative plan is expensive, because
      1. New facilities must be built
      2. New workers have to be trained
      3. New equipment must be purchased

B. These funds will be found by cutting funds for care of the
    poor and elderly
    1. Weak political constituencies get their funding cut first
    2. The poor and the elderly are weak political constituencies
C. These funding cuts will cause harms
    1. Welfare cuts to the poor will harm children in these
        families
    2. Medicare cuts to the elderly will make it more difficult for
        them to get needed medical care

Structure Beyond the Outline

In a debate, you initially present your issues in an outline. However, in
critiquing arguments or in applying certain issues to the other team's positions you might want to use some other techniques. Here are two other
ways of doing so.

1. *List of reasons.* Use numbers: often debaters will provide a list of in-
    dependent reasons why something is or is not true. If the affirmative
    claims that X is harmful, the negative could come up with 1, 2, 3,
    and 4 independent arguments why this is not true. Thus, opponents
    would have to answer each of these separately.
2. *Chain of reasoning.* Use letters: often arguments are more complex
    than one idea and involve several steps. These can be thought of as
    chains of reasoning. Thus, a debater would say that A is true, and B
    is true, and, therefore, this leads to conclusion C. Like any chain, it is
    only as strong as its weakest link. Thus, opponents would only have
    to break the chain at one point.

It is very important to be able to tell the difference between situations
where arguments in a list are independent and where there is a chain of
reasoning. If lists of arguments are launched against a certain point, you
need to address all of them. If there is a chain of reasoning, you only need

to break the chain at some point. If you organize arguments by number and letter you will always be able to tell the difference easily.

Building a Single Argument—The A-R-E Model

A debate is composed of many individual arguments, each of which must be carefully organized. One of the simplest and most effective ways to organize an argument is to use the A-R-E Model, which reflects the way you make an argument in everyday conversation. Using this organization, each argument has three components: the assertion, the reasoning, and the evidence.

A = Assertion. This is the label you give your argument; it is what you want the judge to write down on her flow. The assertion should be relatively short, snappily worded, and express an argumentative relationship between two ideas.

For example, Citizens do not want to pay higher taxes.

R = Reasoning. This is where you explain the logical basis of your argument. It is this component that differentiates a claim from an argument. A claim merely states that something is so, an argument explains why.

For example, Surveys show they do not want to pay for even successful new programs.

E = Evidence. Here is where you use some fact, expert opinion, or logical principle to bolster the point you are making. Evidence must be relevant and directly support your assertion.

For example, New York Times, 11/25/2006: "A Gallup poll released today showed that a taxpayer revolt is in full swing. 85% opposed increasing taxes for new government programs even if the programs themselves would be beneficial."

PUT THEM TOGETHER WITH NOTATION

Remember to keep the components of the argument in order and to precede each assertion label with a number or letter as indicated above, depending on whether you have a list of reasons or a causal chain of ideas. Here is an example:

1. Citizens oppose higher taxes. [A]

2. Surveys show they do not want to pay for even successful new programs. [R]

3. *New York Times*, 11/25/2006: "A Gallup poll released today showed that a taxpayer revolt is in full swing. 85% opposed increasing taxes for new government programs even if the programs themselves would be beneficial." [E]

Signposting—Staying Organized during Your Speech

When driving, you get lost if the signs aren't clear and easy to follow. The same is true while debating. The best way to ensure that the judge understands the order in which you address issues is signposting. You tell the judge that you are leaving one segment of the arguments and are now dealing with another. These transitions also help the judge to follow the order in which you move from issue to issue. Signposting is helpful not only to the other team and to the judge, but also to your partner. Having a coherent discussion of the issues will help the debate move more smoothly and allow more clash with the other team.

When signposting, you might refer to the location of your arguments on your flowsheets. You should tell the judge which flowsheet page you are on, and then refer to where you are on that flowsheet. It is important that the judge understand both on-case and off-case arguments, so make sure the judge is following you.

On-Case (the original affirmative case). These are arguments on the flow pages that begin with the 1AC. They are used to prove or disprove the stock issues of inherency, significance, and solvency. On-case arguments tend to be defensive negative arguments, tearing down what the affirmative has built.

Off-Case. These are negative arguments that do not directly refute the case arguments of inherency, significance, and solvency. They are usually disadvantages, counterplans, topicality arguments, or critiques. Off-case arguments tend to be offensive, building independent reasons to reject the case.

Roadmap your speech to help the judge follow you. This allows the judges and the other team to know which major arguments will be addressed in what order. Roadmapping is:

- Usually done at the beginning of the speech for the judges and the other team
- Usually done in the order of off-case and then on-case arguments

Here are a few examples of how various speakers might roadmap:

1NC: "I will handle the three off-case and then the case debate."

2AC: This speaker will identify the off-case arguments that will be answered first, then the case. "I will cover the China relations disadvantage, the realism critique, and then go to the case arguments."

2NC: Since the 2NC will usually extend some of the off-case arguments, the 2NC usually identifies the specific off-case arguments in the sequence that they will be discussed. "I will deal with the topicality argument and then the China relations disadvantage."

Signposting as described above is very important for the judge. It allows the judge and other teams to identify the specific argument being addressed within each major argument. The judge can then write down your response next to the argument that is being answered.

- Signposting is done throughout each speech; this requires distinguishing between each argument and labeling each argument.

- In signposting, usually numbers and letters are used, but debaters might also use other forms of distinguishing between each argument.
- Examples include: "One. Not-Unique. Present policies will cause the disad. Two. No link. The plan does not cause the disadvantage. Three. Turn. The plan solves the impact to the disad." Debaters can substitute the word "next" in place of specific numbers, but the important thing to do is post a sign which indicates that the next thing you are about to say is a different argument. This will notify the judge and the opponent to record each argument and not miss your brilliance. However, if at all possible, avoid "next" and use numbers.

Transitions are also important for a judge because they provide information about where you are on the flow, while also giving the judge time to organize her flows. Transitions address the way that you move from one off-case argument to another or between the off-case and on-case. For example:
- Often in the 1NC, you will read one disadvantage, and when moving to a second one, you should say, "Next off-case."
- When moving from the off-case to the on-case, you should say, "Now, on the case debate."

Organizing Your Refutation

Organizing your refutation is vital. If you just randomly answer the other team's arguments, the judge might get confused about which argument you are refuting, or if you are offering a new argument for your team. To organize your refutation, use a simple four-step model, each step of which you introduce by a word or phrase:
1. "They say": repeat the short title of the argument you will refute. "They say #3 that U.S. relations with China are bad now . . ."
2. "We disagree": Use this phrase to indicate that you will refute the argument.

3. "Because": present your argument or arguments. If you want to offer more than one reason, number them 1, 2, 3, etc. "Because a strong pattern of trade between the United States and China guarantees that minor disagreements will never grow to threaten these mutually valuable economic relations."
4. "Therefore": indicate what importance "because" has to a larger issue and/or the debate as a whole. "Therefore, any added disagreement about the affirmative plan will not threaten the overall U.S.–China relationship."

When you are organized you keep everyone else organized and ensure that they know which arguments you are talking about. And you vastly increase the chances that your arguments will be noticed and properly applied!

12

Preparing as a Team

You don't debate by yourself; you debate as a team. So, if you are to succeed, you need to prepare as a team. This chapter offers some simple advice on how you can do this. When you begin to debate, it can be a daunting task, with a long list of things to do and prepare. If you establish a productive working relationship with your partner you can divide up or share some tasks, making it much easier to do the work required to succeed.

Partnerships

Your relationship with your partner is an important component of success. If you are incompatible, you will have difficulty winning debates. You and your partner should discuss the following important questions to make sure you are a good match.

- What are your goals in debating?
- How many tournaments do you want to attend? (Have a calendar available and commit to specific dates.)
- Do you have time in your schedules when you are both free to work together?
- How will you deal with adversity and frustration?
- How do you deal with winning and losing?

- What are your perceived weaknesses and strengths as debaters? You may not be sure yet, and your analysis may change, but you should address the question in your initial discussions.

You should also come to an agreement on the following issues:
- Speaker positions. There are four speaker positions in the debate (1A, 2A, 1N, 2N). It is often best to have one person be the second affirmative and the other person the second negative. This way you can share responsibilities, each for a side.
- Division of labor. Who will do how much research, how much briefing, how much preparation of arguments, etc.
- Acquisition of needed items. Who will get the supplies you need, such as folders, evidence containers, flow paper, etc.

How to Prepare on the Affirmative

Your first step is determining who will be in charge of the side. Traditionally, because the second affirmative speaker (A2) gives two very important unscripted speeches while the first affirmative speaker reads a prepared script, the second affirmative is in charge. Of course, the first affirmative will help, but the second affirmative should guide and plan the major preparation tasks. To ease the burden of preparation, it helps if the team members split the second positions on different sides of the topic.

Here are some important steps in preparing the affirmative:
- Work together to decide which affirmative case to use and prepare the first affirmative speech. Order the evidence, label the arguments, write the plan, and think about strategy. The 1A should then practice and time the speech.
- Together make a list of the most common arguments against your case. Use your own ideas but also ask other squad members what sorts of arguments they face.

- Because the 2A has the responsibility of defending the case and answering negative arguments, she should
  - prepare preliminary frontline answers to each of the anticipated negative arguments
  - prepare to defend each word in the topic against topicality attacks by making sure the team has its own definition for each word and can justify it
  - gather and organize all of the evidence and prepared arguments to use to defend the case. Often, when you receive evidence from institutes, handbooks, etc., the answers to the negative arguments will also be included. Be sure to organize answers to all of the more generic negative arguments separately.
- Hold abbreviated practice debates. Have the 1AC pick some arguments that an imaginary negative team has used, and have the 2AC address them. Change the negative strategy and repeat it again.

How to Prepare on the Negative

Just as the 2A takes the majority of the responsibility on the affirmative, the 2N takes more of the responsibility on the negative. The first negative will help, of course, but the second negative can guide and plan the major preparation tasks. Once again, it helps if the two team members have split the second positions on different sides of the topic.

Here are some important steps in preparing the negative:

- *Make sure you have all your negative arguments that are available.* Target specific areas of research. Think about the most common affirmative cases on the topic as well as where you are weak for planning this effort.
- *Compare with other teams, trade, cooperate, and try to increase the number of different negative approaches you have.*
- *Have a separate section in your filing system for each of your major negative arguments,* such as disadvantages, critiques, counterplans, and topicality

arguments as well as evidence and arguments against specific cases. Make them easy to get and use by putting the individual arguments in the separate categories.

- *Create folders for the negative arguments you expect to use the most,* such as disadvantages, critiques, and the like, or organize them in expando/ accordion files. Label the folders and organize them in some logical way, either by the name of the argument or by type of argument (all of the disadvantage folders in one section, all of the critique folders in another, etc.) Most arguments can just be put in separate folders. However, organize arguments that you may use frequently in separate sections of an expando/accordion file with an index taped to the front.
- *Find the best 8–10 pieces of evidence to extend each of your major negative arguments.*
- *Create folders for negative arguments you have against specific cases.* Often when you receive evidence from institutes, handbooks, etc., the negative answers to the affirmative cases you are not using will also be included. Pull these answers and put them in your negative materials, each in a folder with the case name on it. No matter how you receive evidence, make sure to organize it not just by argument, but by affirmative or negative. You will always be on one side or the other.
- *Make a separate topicality file with prepared violations and definitions clearly separated.*
- Once you have these materials organized, *make a list of the most common affirmative cases used by other teams and prepare negative strategies to use against them.*

Your experience in working together as a debate team is a marvelous preparation for your later life when you will find yourself in many situations in which you will be required to cooperate to succeed. Be kind and tolerant toward your debate partner, because without a partner you cannot compete. Sharing the burdens of preparation can make your overall relationship easier.

13

Cross-Examination

The cross-examination period of a debate is a time when the person who is not going to speak next in the constructives questions the person who has just finished speaking. Consider cross-examination an information exchange period—it is not the time to role-play lawyer.

Objectives of Cross-Examination

Cross-examination has six objectives:
1. To clarify points
2. To expose errors
3. To obtain admissions
4. To set up arguments
5. To save prep time
6. To show the judge that you are an intelligent, polite person so she will want to vote for you

Most debaters underestimate the value of good cross-examination. But remember that it is an essential part of the debate; 20% of time is spent in it. Cross-examination can have an important impact on the judge. Because it is spontaneous, cross-examination will indicate to the judge just how sharp the debaters are. And judges always like the sharpest team to win. Good, effective cross-examination plays an important psychological role in winning the ballot of the judge.

Whenever you cross-examine, be dynamic. Have your questions ready, and answer questions with confidence. The image you project is very important to the judge. Cross-examination is the one opportunity the judge has to compare you and your opponent, literally side-by-side, since this is the only time in the debate you will be standing next to your opponent.

Guidelines for Asking Questions

Too often new debaters just ask random questions during cross-examination without thinking about how to use questions to advance their side. Here are some suggestions for asking questions appropriately and strategically.

- *Ask a question designed to get a* short *answer.* This type of question is far more direct and efficient. Do not ask, "How does your plan work"; ask, "What specific mechanism solves this problem?"
- *Indicate the object of your question.* Make a reference to a specific argument or piece of evidence. Do not say, "You have some evidence about taxation . . ."; say, "On your evidence from the *New York Times* about taxation . . ."
- *Don't telegraph your argument.* Don't make it too obvious. You can't trap someone if he sees it coming. Do not say, "We will prove your plain fails . . ."; say, "So, you show attitudinal inherency by indicating that people do not want this solution, correct?" Then you can argue later that they will not cooperate with the implementation of the plan.
- *Don't ask questions that no sensible debater would answer the way you want.* For example, do not ask, "So, we win, right?" They are not going to admit any such thing.

- *Make a question seem important.* Even if it is just an attempt to clarify, make sure the question appears significant. For example, say, "Can you explain the logic behind X," instead of "Can you explain X; I do not understand." In this case, you want to indicate that the problem is your opponent's expression of this idea, not your inability to understand.
- *Be polite.* If your opponent becomes rude, become more polite. You want the judge to notice the difference.
- *Approach issues from a non-obvious direction to develop a trap.* For example, don't ask questions like, "This will cost a lot of money, right?" Instead, ask questions like, "How can you possibly put together the administrative structure to implement this plan?" and then use the answer to prove that the plan will be expensive.
- *Avoid open-ended questions.* Unless you are sure your opponent will not be able to answer them, stay away from them. For example, don't say, "Can you tell me why this disadvantage is untrue?" Otherwise you are just inviting your opponent to give a speech for her team during your question time.
- *Face the judge, not your opponent.* Watch her for non-verbal reactions.
- *Integrate your opponent's answers into your arguments.* You score points by using the opposition's answers in your speech to support your arguments.

Guidelines for Answering Questions

Some beginning debaters answer questions without thinking strategically. Think about how your answer might be used against you. However, you don't want to appear uncooperative—judges dislike that. Answer the question, but be strategic. Here are some basic suggestions for answering questions:

- *Whenever possible, give a concise answer.* It makes you appear in control of the issues. And often, when you give short answers, your opponents will run out of good questions.
- *Whenever possible, refer to something specific you have already said.* This cannot get you into trouble because you've already said it. Answers such as, "As our *New York Times* evidence indicated in the B sub-point . . ." shows the judge that you are familiar with your speech and that the answer was there all along but your opponent didn't hear it. This type of answer helps you avoid making dangerous mistakes by rambling on about some issue.
- *Answer based on your position in the debate so far.* Keep options open. Say things like, "As of this point in the debate . . ." and then refer to a statement you already made.
- *Don't promise to present evidence or explain a statement in a later speech.* Present the requested information when asked.
- *Qualify your answers.* This will make them seem more realistic. Instead of "all," say "almost all" or "most."
- *Be willing to offer the opposition documents read into the debate, but don't show documents that you have not yet introduced.*
- *Answer only questions relevant to the debate.* Questions that seem unrelated may be designed to trap you. Decline to answer questions you deem irrelevant. If your opponent demands an answer, first ask how the question is relevant.
- *Address the judge.* Watch for her non-verbal reactions.
- *Don't answer hypothetical questions.* These are often attempts to trap you. If your opponent demands an answer, say you will give a hypothetical answer only if he proves something first. For example, answer a question such as, "When there is a revolution in Iran and a new government takes over, won't that mean your proposal will not work?" by saying, "First prove that there is going to be a revolution in Iran, and then we can address this issue."
- *Signal each other.* If you are seated, don't answer the question being asked of your partner unless you are sure the judge does not mind

this tactic. Many judges strongly dislike team cross-examination. If your opponent is cross-examining you and you do not know how to answer a question, your seated partner might signal discreetly (palm open up means "yes," palm open down means "no").

- *Don't say, "I don't know."* Instead say, "I am not sure at this time." That way you can answer later in rebuttal.

Tactics for Specific Cross-Examination Situations

Here are some tactics that each speaker might consider during her cross-examination.

2NC Cross-Examination of 1AC

Get missing signposts and arguments:

- Center most of your questions on the plan. Look for plan errors and possible links to disadvantages. Ask for a copy of the plan and read it.
- Make sure that you understand the thesis of the case and what advantages are being claimed. If you are not sure, ask. Now is the time to do it, not after the 2AC!

1AC Cross-Examination of 1NC

Explore the opposition's arguments for possible weaknesses:

- If the 1NC argued topicality, make sure that you know what the violations claimed are and what standards the opposition is using to prove that you are not topical. Ask her what you have to do to meet her definition. Your opponent will often give you an example of how you can answer this argument.
- Make the 1NC explain any arguments that you do not understand.
- Ask the 1NC explain the links, thresholds, and/or impacts to the disadvantages that she argued.

- Ask the 1NC to explain why the counterplan is better than the plan or will actually solve the affirmative harm. Ask her to compare specific quantifiable disadvantages and advantages.

1NC Cross-Examination of 2AC and 2AC Cross-Examination of 2NC
Ask for any responses that your partner missed.
- Ask for any briefs or evidence that you or your partner need in order to answer every response given by the 2AC/2NC.
- Ask the 2AC/2NC to explain why he or she may have conceded some arguments—especially on advantages or disadvantages.

14

*Research**

Policy debating stands in contrast to other debate forms, such as parliamentary or extemporaneous debate, because it calls on the participants to use substantial bodies of research in the debate. It has, at times, been referred to as a "contest between teams with oral term papers," in which references and direct quotations from experts, scholars, and news sources are used to explain and support arguments. Policy debating requires participants to research a single controversy deeply and become familiar with the facts, theories, and perspectives published on it. This creates research skills and habits that can pay rich dividends later in life.

The Importance of Research

Contemporary policy debate, both in high school and college, is largely research driven. In policy debate we process enormous amounts of information in order to discuss important issues. Consequently, our capacity to do research has a great deal to do with our success in debate.

---

*I want to thank Pat Gehrke (http://www.cas.sc.edu/engl/faculty/faculty_pages/gehrke/gehrke.html) of the University of South Carolina for his ideas and assistance with this section.

Each of us must find our own perspective in the political arena, and research helps us to do that. By learning to find and utilize the most relevant information on a topic, we find how we can argue an issue in our own way. When we speak out on issues, each of us speaks in her or his own voice, yet we need to be familiar with all the facts, theories, and opinions surrounding the topic in order to be truly persuasive.

Research is also essential to being an effective advocate in our society. We speak of our information age, ruled by an information economy, and in which we fight information wars. Consequently, the control and management of information has become a critical element of political effectiveness. A person who cannot effectively make use of information—find it, read it, organize it, and talk about it—is a person who is not an effective participant in society. Information is power.

A Debate Research Plan

Policy debaters begin their research not by doing but by thinking: what information do we need and how will we find it? You have to plan before you begin your research. Here are some basic tips on researching successfully.

- *Have a strategic focus.* Know what you are looking for so that you can best focus on finding what you really need. You will approach your research much differently if you are looking for a very recent quotation about the president's popularity than if you are looking for material that analyzes the connection between presidential popularity and the implementation of public policies the president supports.
- *Sketch out the arguments you will use and determine the evidence you will need to support them.* Be imaginative and flexible. Research may lead you in different directions, so you may have to adapt your position as you go along.
- *Develop a research plan.* Never embark on your research project without a relatively clear plan of action. Begin by making a list of the research

resources you think might be useful. Do not forget about the people you might contact to help you begin your research. Think about the libraries to which you have access and the print and electronic materials they might provide for you. Also think about what Web resources might be helpful.

- *Prioritize your research.* Rank the research avenues open to you from most to least useful. Always begin with those resources that can help you focus your initial research. Conversations with teachers, professors, coaches, and organizations should be the first step in your plan. Then consult general sources to locate your argument. A preliminary Web search might be a good way to survey possible ideas. Review periodicals before books, as they provide faster access to needed information and may be more current. Review the full-text databases before the citation-only indexes, since the whole content will be instantly available instead of having to search for it. As your research progresses, consult books for in-depth information as well as citation indexes, which might lead you to additional resources.
- *Budget your research time.* Think about how much time you can devote to the research project and how that time should be spent. Even experienced researchers often will underestimate how much time they need to read and process evidence. One general rule is to split research time 30/70, with 30% assigned to retrieving material and 70% devoted to absorbing that material. Your split will depend on what type of research, reading, and processing skills you develop. Whatever you decide, build in extra time, often as much as 10–15%.

Library Resources

GAINING ACCESS

Library resources vary depending on the population a library serves. A small neighborhood library or a high school library does not have the resources a research or university library has. Getting access to a research or academic library will help you expand your research considerably. You can usually gain access in one of three ways.

1. *Ask the library.* Some libraries will open their doors to the public, even if they might not permit general borrowing. Many university libraries do not restrict access, and those that do may have an arrangement with your school permitting you access. In some cases, librarians will let you use their facilities if you explain that you are a debater researching this year's national topic.

2. *Ask your coach, principal, librarian, or other official to work out a special arrangement for your access to the library.* Sometimes university libraries provide access to anyone with a legitimate research interest if he or she submits a letter from a school official requesting access and explaining the need.

3. *Buy access.* You frequently can use a university library for a fee ranging from $10 to $50 dollars a year. Given the hundreds of thousands, if not millions, of dollars worth of information that even a mediocre university library provides, the fee is probably worth it.

REFERENCE MATERIALS

The reference section in most libraries can be extremely helpful as a beginning of your research. You can use the reference section to examine resources such as dictionaries of various types and specialties, encyclopedias both broad and targeted, almanacs with various sorts of statistical data, atlases and maps, short histories, indexes to periodicals, social science and citation indexes, and many other reference works. In addition, the reference librarian can guide you to other resources.

ONLINE RESOURCES

The librarian can provide you with a list of the various online resources to which the library has access. Online resources are huge depositories of information that you can search easily to find the full text of suitable articles. Using this research tool can save you valuable time, and you can download articles for future reference. You may have to pay a fee for using these resources, but most libraries will allow you access to a number of full-text data bases without payment.

Some of the best on-line resources for debaters include the following:

LexisNexis

LexisNexis is the most useful online resource for current events and legal research. It contains huge numbers of full-text articles from newspapers, magazines, newsletters, wire services, law journals, and medical journals. Because its holdings are so big, you will need to use the power search available at the interface to take full advantage of this resource.

Expanded Academic Index ASAP

This is an excellent database of popular and scholarly literature. Most of the material is full text, and this service allows a variety of delivery options, including e-mail. In the search terms entry box, you will find two options: subject and keyword. Always use keyword.

JSTOR

This service offers a wide variety of scholarly journals and publications that can't be found on LexisNexis. This system has some good search functions. You can select what part of the citation or article you want to search, and you can connect terms using the pull-down menus for "and," "or," "near" (10), and near (25). You also can select date limitations. Regardless of these other functions, you must select what journals to search in and what type of material should be included. I recommend that you generally default to searching all the journals and include all the types of material.

Periodicals

Debates and periodicals have an important thing in common—current events. Debates tend to be about what is happening now and so do a wide variety of news magazines. You can usually examine these through LexisNexis, but if you do not have access to that service, you should consult the *Reader's Guide to Periodical Literature* in the reference section of the library. Many periodicals eventually are bound and shelved, but you usually can find the most recent volumes in the periodical reading room. If you find a reference to an article that is not in the library's collection, the librarian can usually order a copy for you.

BOOKS

Books are important for exploring a topic in depth, but because your time is limited, you have to use them wisely. Choose those that seem most relevant (based on their subtitles) and most recent. First review the table of contents and then the index to see if the book will be helpful. Then review only the chapters you think important, reading the beginning and end of each chapter and then skimming the subtitles and topic sentences to find what you want quickly. Check out those that look best but don't get carried away by taking too many volumes.

GOVERNMENT DOCUMENTS

Many libraries have depositories of U.S. government documents that can be very useful. You can also use the "Thomas" Web service (http://www.thomas.gov), but many libraries still have hard copies. Very current government documents usually cover existing controversies in a useful way that you can take advantage of. In a congressional hearing about a certain issue, those representing the various sides will testify and potential laws are discussed in terms of pros and cons. The Government Accounting Office has a number of excellent studies about recent issues that are balanced and well documented. Each department of government has its own publications.

INTERNET RESEARCH

Policy debaters tend to use the Internet extensively for research. Some believe that debaters rely too heavily on the Internet, and in response to this some teams will use arguments that they believe are not easily researched on the Internet. You can't be a thorough researcher by simply sitting at a computer and doing a search. You will need to follow many research paths to do an excellent job. Nevertheless, the Internet can be an important resource—if you use it wisely.

Use Internet information with caution. Anyone can put up information on the Web, and some unqualified person can launch any unsupported theory. For an example of this, you might visit the Flat Earth Society at http://www.alaska.net/~clund/e_djublonskopf/Flatearthsociety.htm or the Church of the Subgenius at http://www.subgenius.com, although the latter takes itself somewhat less seriously than the former. You have to determine who has written the information you find and to apply questions of expertise and authority to them. The Internet has a lot of information, but you must evaluate it critically.

Most people use Internet search engines to find information they are looking for. These search engines come and go, and some are very specific. They use different methodologies to gather answers to your questions. It is a good idea to consult Search Engine Watch at http://searchengine-watch.com/links/ for guidance.

The most popular search engine at the time of this writing is Google at http://www.google.com. The "power search" and "Google Scholar" features can be very useful. Other popular search engines are Yahoo at http://www.yahoo.com because it has a directory system you can navigate your way through to find things you otherwise would miss. Ask.com at http://www.ask.com is also useful because it allows you to ask questions and tries to give you answers.

Other search engines use different methodologies. Mooter at http://www.mooter.com gives you bundles of answers that are relevant to each other, allowing you to select from context and find relevant information sooner. Rollyo at http://www.rollyo.com allows you to build your own search engine for a specific topic or use a search engine that one of its many expert users has created. Both of these are interesting and innovative options to the more mainstream search engines.

You can limit the number of irrelevant results you receive by using the various special features on the specific search engine you use. However, always use a critical lens on such information.

Several Web sites allow policy debaters to purchase extensive evidence files. While I do not approve of these because they treat evidence as a commodity and do not encourage debaters to hone their research skills, they are a fact of life in policy debate. These sites and services include the following:

Big Sky Debate at http://research.bigskydebate.com/debate-resources/sample-books/

Communican National Debate Handbook at http://www.communican.org/c/products/national_debate_handbook.asp

Cross-X.com at http://www.cross-x.com

Debate Central at http://debate.uvm.edu/eebooks.html

Planet Debate at http://www.planetdebate.com

West Coast Publishing http://www.wcdebate.com

15

Evidence

I have heard that during a year of policy debate the average debater will do as much work as would be associated with a thesis or dissertation. But as many graduate students can tell you, there is a difference between finding the raw information through the research process and turning it into useful information. This chapter explains how to turn your research into evidence that supports specific arguments.

Creating Evidence Cards

Research is just the first step. Now you have to extract the specific information you want to use to support your arguments from your research and organize it. You do this through a process called cutting evidence. You take the specific paragraph you want to use to support your argument out of the larger text, affix it to a piece of paper, add the complete citation, and then label the paper as evidence supporting some specific argument you would like to make in its tagline, which is the debater's term for a short version of the precise argument being made by the evidence. Debaters also refer to evidence as "cards," since some time ago evidence was put on index cards; now it is usually put onto briefed pages, pages that can contain more than one related argument. However, calling a piece of evidence a "card" remains part of policy debate jargon.

There are several main things to remember as you begin the process of creating evidence:

- *Cut mostly cards that make arguments.* If it does not make an argument, you are not likely to use it. There is definitely a place for informational cards, but they should be labeled as such so they're not used inappropriately in rounds.
- *Never cut one-sentence cards.* They rarely make a real argument. Cut the entire paragraph so you have a context for the author's ideas.
- *Cards should be complete thoughts.* In other words, you need complete sentences (cards should begin with a capital letter and end with a punctuation mark).
- *Don't cut cards that aren't what the author advocates.* This includes cards where the word after the material you've clipped is "but."

Simple Guidelines for Evidence Citation

Evidence should always include a complete citation. Just as scholarly articles and term papers cite sources, debaters should make it possible for others to identify where evidence comes from. Include the following information in your citations:

a. The author
b. The author's qualifications
c. The date of the publication
d. The publication—book title, journal and article title, etc.
e. The page number of the original quotation

Unacceptable:

Wade 99 or New York Times 99 or Senate Hearings 99

Acceptable:

Melissa Wade, Adjunct Education Professor, Emory Univ., Fall 1999 *Journal of Debate Love*, "Great African American Debaters," p. 23

The rules for citation don't change when citing the Web. You must still include the following: author, qualification, publication, date, and a *full* Web site address. Citing "Schoolinfo.com" or "Internet" as a source is not acceptable. If you can't find the full cite for a source from the net, don't use the evidence.

You should also become familiar with the National Forensic League's standards for evidence citation. They can be found here: http://www. nflonline.org/uploads/AboutNFL/ntman07.pdf.

Evaluating Evidence

Debaters use the best evidence they have to support the arguments that they wish to present. This is understandable, because there is no such thing as "perfect evidence," nor is there one sort of evidence that is always better than others. The criteria one uses to determine the quality of the evidence changes with each argument and its associated claim. However, here are some general criteria for evaluating the evidence that you will use or that the opposing team has presented.

- *The evidence should support the claim you are making in the argument.* It should do more than just infer the claim or allude to it: it should directly support it.
- *The evidence should give strong reasons why the claim is true.* If a newspaper article says that next time the Democrats will win the presidency without explaining why, it is probably inadequate. A good argument must give warrants: reasons why the argument should be accepted.
- *The evidence should be strongly worded.* It should suggest that something "probably" or "definitely" will happen—instead of "might" or "possibly could" happen. The stronger the wording the better.
- *The evidence should come from a qualified source.* The reason you use evidence to prove arguments is because you are not a subject-area expert. Evidence should come from qualified and respected sources. Evaluate the author of your evidence for formal training and education, experience

in the field, affiliation with some respected organization, or a good track record of evaluating and predicting events. Always include qualifications in your citation.

- *The evidence should be appropriately recent.* This is particularly important when dealing with topics that are changing rapidly. You would want a piece of evidence claiming that China and the United States are on the brink of a breakdown in relations because of human rights criticisms to be very recent. On the other hand, a piece of more philosophical evidence about the dangers of mixing church and state need not be recent. Always include the complete date on all citations.

Evidence Drills

Learning how to work with, utilize, and critique evidence is an important skill. Here are some simple exercises you can do to improve your ability to criticize and utilize evidence. These are best done with a small group of team members.

1. In a small group, take several pieces of evidence and have a contest to see how many faults you can find with it. List the faults and pick the best three criticisms.
2. Find two pieces of evidence that say the opposite thing. Come up with reasons why each is better than the other, and then decide which really is better evidence.
3. Find a short newspaper article that has some relevance to your topic. You and your teammates can individually read the article, bracket the evidence, and then write out taglines for each piece of evidence you find. Compare what you find.
4. Look at a contention from your first affirmative speech, or better yet from an opponent's first affirmative speech (or a disadvantage, or a counterplan—whatever you want to work on) and criticize the evidence.

16

Briefing

When a debater has enough evidence to make a fairly complete argument, she organizes the evidence onto "briefs" for easy storage, retrieval, and use. (You can see a sample brief in Appendix 3.) A brief is a short organized argument with evidence prepared in advance of a debate for quick reference. Just as an essay or a research paper would present a well-supported argument, so a debate speech must do the same through the presentation of briefs. Briefing is a complex intellectual task, but one that you will find rewarding in your debate career as well as beneficial in the long run.

Here is a sample from the brief in Appendix 3:

3. TRADITIONAL DEMOCRATIC THEORY FAILS [tagline]
Carol C. Gould, Prof. Philosophy, Stevens Inst. of Tech., RETHINK-ING DEMOCRACY, 1990, p. 3. [citation]

The premise of this book is that there is a need for a new theory of democracy and for a rethinking of its philosophical foundations. This need derives, in the first instance, from the inadequacies of the traditional democratic theory of liberal individualism, which, despite the strength of its emphasis on individual liberty, fails to take sufficiently into account the requirements of social cooperation and social equality. [body of evidence quotation]

Titles and Tagging of Briefs

Each brief page has a title explaining what is on that brief, and each piece of evidence (card) has a tagline that explains the argument that the evidence supports. The titles and tags must reflect the content of the evidence. Make sure that the briefs are legible and easy to use for your fellow debaters, who will need to use them quickly during the debate.

Writing Briefs and Taglines

Briefs that include tagged evidence are materials that you often construct outside of the round and before the tournament. Here are some general guidelines to keep in mind when developing this material.

- The tagline introduces the evidence and tells the judge the argument that the evidence supports. Therefore, when writing the taglines, don't overstate the evidence or claim that it says things that it doesn't.
- Do not simply restate the card. Turn it into a debate argument. For example, on a renewable energy topic, "High cost prevents renewable energy use" is better than "can't solve."
- Do not curse or use street language on the brief or the tags. The judge may ask to see them after the debate.
- Do not use symbols or excessive abbreviations anywhere on the brief. Your teammates may not understand them, and it could hurt them in a debate.
- Whenever possible type out the tag. If you must handwrite a tag, do so neatly. Other people must be able to read your tag easily.

Format of Brief Pages

Briefs must be constructed so that it is immediately obvious what they are for and how to use them. They should also be constructed so that they can be easily organized. Here are some guidelines for formatting your briefs.

- Put the school name (or institute name) and your name in the upper left corner of the page.
- Note the general argument area. For example, Spending Disadvantage, costly plan causes other cuts.
- Place the page number of the brief and extent of pages in the upper right corner (if you have three pages stating why the plan would be unpopular, there should be a page 1 of 3, 2 of 3, and 3 of 3).
- Don't put numbers by the taglines above the cards, so numbers can be inserted during a debate round. By the tag of each card, put a (__) for the team to insert a number during the debate. You may pick one piece of evidence from a page to use in a debate, so a number (as if you were reading the entire page) can be confusing.

Taping Briefs

Now you are ready to attach the evidence cards to the brief page that you have constructed. Usually this is done with transparent plastic tape. Tape all of the corners of the cards down!

- This includes the citation that should be taped to the card and then taped to the page on both corners.
- Use only clear tape, no glue sticks or an alternate method of sticking.
- Leave one inch all around the edge of the page, so you can have a footer and decent margins.
- Get as much on one page as you can, to ease the copying burden, but don't get carried away with cramming.

Strategic Considerations—Or How to Make Your Work More Useful

You have put together some argument briefs, and now you need to organize them in a meaningful way so that you can find the information you need easily and quickly. To do so, take related briefs and put them together in a file that is organized logically. Here are some guidelines for turning individual briefs into a file of briefs.

- For big arguments that the entire team will use, write a summary explaining the argument and how to use the evidence in the file. Then create a table of contents, listing titles and page numbers in the brief.
- Put the best briefs in the front of the file and the best cards at the top of each brief, so that they are easily accessible under the time constraints of the round.
- Include analytical arguments as well as cards on the brief. Using a combination of analytical arguments and cards is far more effective than just reading lots of evidence, because it focuses the argumentation on crucial key points.
- Be aware that there might be contradictions or interactions with other cards on the briefs.
- Don't spread a card over two pages. This will only serve to confuse others trying to use your evidence and might confuse you in the pressure of a debate.
- Don't shrink text down too much. Avoid too much reduction when photocopying articles and books.

Analytical Arguments

Some arguments are "analytical" because they do not have a formal evidence component. These arguments are instances of common logic and common information being applied to what the other team is saying. You can often "analyze" the arguments you have briefed and therefore anticipate what opponents will say. If you do not have a brief, you can always use your analysis to develop arguments that can substitute for a brief. A purely analytical argument would not have format evidence cards associated with it, but it can still be a powerful form of argument. Evidence is nice to have, but the argument is still the most important element.

Analysis Drills

Learning to analyze and critique arguments is an essential part of debating. Here are some exercises that might prove useful. These are usually best done with a small group of debaters.

Case analysis. Take a sample contention from a 1AC and find flaws in the argument. It could be a contention from your affirmative, it could be a contention from an affirmative used by one of your main opponents, or it could be one a teammate made up with flaws hidden in it.

Disadvantage analysis. Take a sample disadvantage and find answers to it. Focus on disadvantages you hear quite often against your affirmative case.

Topicality analysis. Take a sample plan and some definitions and build a topicality argument. Use your plan, and then map out how you would answer the topicality argument.

Take a briefed argument and cut up the pieces of evidence so that they are no longer associated. Then add several pieces of irrelevant evidence from a different but related argument. Give these to your partner or fellow squad members and have them find the argument and rebuild it.

17

Rebuttals

Most debaters, coaches, and judges would agree that rebuttals are the most difficult and yet the most important parts of the debate. Not only do debaters have less time for their speeches, but they also have to sort through all of the issues to determine which ones are the most important! What a debater does or does not do in rebuttals will decide who wins the debate. Very few debaters (especially beginners) can hope to deal with all the arguments presented in the constructive speeches. Debaters don't have to further advance all arguments, and just because a team may have dropped a point or an argument is not an automatic reason to vote against that team. What matters is the type of argument that is advanced or dropped in rebuttals, as this will determine the winner of the debate.

There are some fairly clear standards one should use when considering which arguments to focus on in the rebuttals. Think about these four issues:

1. Which arguments have more impact? Arguments about the health of millions are more important than arguments about the health of hundreds.
2. Which outcomes (disadvantages, counterplans) are more likely, given lots of internal links in a possibly vulnerable chain of reasoning. The probability of the outcome influences the impact that it will have in the debate.

3. What about time frame—what happens first? Events that come sooner are traditionally thought of as more important than equal events that take place later.
4. What about the quality of evidence? An issue with better and stronger evidence is something that the judge is far more likely to take seriously.

Here are some helpful hints for better rebuttals:

- *Avoid repetition.* Don't just repeat your constructive arguments. Defeat the other team's arguments and tell the judge why your arguments are better.
- *Don't avoid what the other team said.* You must clash directly with the opposition's responses.
- *Avoid reading only evidence.* You must explain why the issues you have chosen win the debate.
- *Avoid rereading evidence presented in constructives.* You can refer to it, but don't repeat it.
- *Avoid "lumping and dumping."* Don't try to win every issue in the debate or even deal with every single idea. You can't make 12 responses to each argument in a few minutes.
- *Be organized.* Don't randomly jump from issue to issue. Be specific and logical about winning issues. Use your flowsheet to guide you.
- *Use issue packages.* Organize your arguments into issue packages. Choose arguments that you want to win. Don't try to cover everything. Extend those arguments that you need to win.
- *Speak quickly but not beyond your ability.* If you speak too fast, you will stumble and not get through as much.
- *Don't whine to the judge about fairness.* Don't complain about what the other team might have done that you think is abusive in their theoretical approach to the debate. Make responses and beat them.
- *Don't make new arguments.* You can read new evidence but you can't offer new disadvantages or topicality responses in rebuttals. You

are limited to extending the positions laid out in the constructive speeches.

- *Use signposting.* Make sure the judge knows where you are on the flow-sheet. This is not the time to lose the judge on the flow.

18

Adapting to Judges and Audiences

Judges, like all of us, are products of their background and experience. They have different perspectives and preferences. To succeed in debating, you must adapt your ideas and strategies to them. This chapter provides you with general tips on adapting to judges and performing in the debate in ways that specific types of judges prefer.

Collecting and Using Information on the Judge

Keep notes on each judge you have had. When they judge you again, you can adapt more effectively. Combine your notes with those of other team members to create a file about all of the judges in your league or tournaments. You can also question other debaters about a judge you have been assigned. Finally, you can ask the judge before the debate to relate her experience and explain her judging philosophy.

Once you have information, you need to use it. Always make assessments about your judge using basic audience analysis concepts:

- Well informed, generally informed, poorly informed about an idea
- Highly motivated, moderately motivated, poorly motivated
- Agrees, no opinion, disagrees with an idea

Remember that the judge is another person listening. She knows less about your argument than you do. You must reach her with your speeches and be clear in your presentation. But she is also:

- Watching the entire debate. Watching you before the round, before you speak, while you are working with your partner, etc. You are under the microscope as soon as you enter the room.
- Comparing you with your opponent. If the opposition does something irritating, make sure you don't. Be strong where the opposition is weak. Make the judge's choice between you and your opponent clear.
- Expecting a dignified and tasteful performance. Be professional and task oriented. Don't be silly, irreverent, or too chummy with the judge or the opposition.
- Interested in the debate, not your ego. Sell the issues, not your desire to win.
- Aware that some of your arguments are better than others, and the same goes for your opponent's. Don't claim to "win everything"; make a realistic and credible call on how things are going.
- Sending non-verbal signals. These can tell you what she likes, what she doesn't like, and whether she is lost or not.
- Correct. It is your job to please her, not the other way around.

Types of Judges

Judges fall into one of three categories based on the role they see themselves in:

Type A: Judge of Academic Debate Contest. This judge is usually a debate coach, a former debater, or someone who judges regularly. She is open minded about debate, works hard during the round, wants to make an unbiased decision, and has decent knowledge of the topic and debate procedures. Her focus is on fair competition.

Type B: Educator Coach of "Learning" Debates. The Type B judge sees the focus of the debate as education more than fair competition. He wants to "teach you" something and you had better be ready to learn. This judge is generally an older or more traditional teacher who also coaches or judges debate. He may have not judged in a while or at your level.

Type C: Esteemed Judge of Entertaining Debates. All judges like to be entertained, but Type C expects you to put on a show, and thus wants to call it a "good debate." This is often a lay judge ("Here's a ballot; go judge a debate"), a judge who is disenchanted with the current form of debate, someone who hasn't judged in a long time, or someone who is burned out as a debate coach and just wants to get through the judging obligation. Make the round enjoyable and make yourself sound articulate and you can win.

Adapting to Specific Judge Types

Each of these judge types requires some specific adaptations. While this text will prepare you for a Type A judge, you may have to make some minor adaptations based on the individual. The other two types do require specific and conscious adaptation.

TYPE B ADAPTATIONS

You will need to make the following adjustments to your debating when dealing with this kind of judge.

Delivery:

- Speak more slowly than usual. Pace your delivery based on his notetaking activities and non-verbal reactions to make sure the judge is engaged.
- Speak in more complete sentences. Don't use fragmentary taglines.

- Give summaries of major arguments (case contentions, disadvantages, etc.) as you finish them.
- Make sure he knows which argument you are talking about. You will need better signposting for pages of the flow. Pause before moving to another major point.
- Watch carefully for non-verbals of agreement/disagreement or understanding/misunderstanding.

Content:

- Give a thesis statement and a more detailed explanation before presenting a major argument in order to create context.
- Avoid debate jargon. Explain debate concepts in words everyone can understand ("link turn" becomes "we solve that problem," while "permutation" becomes "you don't have to vote against us to gain the advantages of the counterplan").
- Give reasons for theoretical requirements instead of assuming that they know about debate theory. Explain why a non-competitive counterplan is "not a reason to vote against our case." Don't just tell the judge to "reject the counterplan because it is not competitive."
- Emphasize the specificity of argumentation less than you would with the Type A judge. The Type B judge is more concerned with the big picture than the precise details.
- Use fewer arguments and issues; develop them more completely.
- Use internal summaries. As you exit an issue, explain why you win it and why it is important before moving on to your next major point.
- Use external, or concluding, summaries. Summarize and weigh the issues carefully at the end of your speech, leaving time to explain their interaction.
- Use less evidence and explain it more.
- Assume the judge accepts the current American conventional wisdom and work from there.

TYPE C ADAPTATIONS

You need to make the following adjustments to your debating when dealing with this kind of judge.

Delivery:

- Do everything you would do for Type B but more so. You should be a bit slower, use more complete sentences, give more examples, etc.
- Be more colorful, and be more complete.
- Develop a finite number of themes and apply them liberally to arguments in the debate.
- Focus on major points only, not on smaller specific arguments, although you must not be perceived as ignoring issues.
- Create the impression that you and the judge understand what is going on and the other team does not.

Content:

- Do everything you would do for Type B but more so. Develop single arguments more; don't use debate jargon, and so on.
- Focus on major concepts and ideas. Make an extra effort to explain *how* an argument or idea works.
- Assume the current conventional wisdom and stay there. Avoid radical ideas.
- Explain all theory issues such as topicality and counterplan competition as being "logically required" and then explain why. On competition, for example, say, "Since you do not have to choose between the counterplan and our plan, the counterplan is not a reason to reject our affirmative case."
- Use fewer pieces of evidence, emphasize qualifications, and focus on reasons given inside the evidence.
- Don't use jargon at all. Replace it with everyday words.
- Realize that the judge will not so much vote on the issues as decide who should win and then sort the issues out based on that. The overall impression is essential.

Part Four

Endless Journey

The experience of policy debating is an endless journey. Your experience of this format will never be finalized, and even after many years of active participation, there is always something new to be learned and always a new set of skills to be refined and redefined. This section offers more advanced materials that will help you once you've learned the basics.

19

The Better Debater?

I was asked by a number of New York Urban Debate League coaches to develop a list of characteristics I would assign to the "better" debater as well as those I would assign to the "not better" debater. Since a debate is won by the team that did the "better job of debating," these characteristics very often translate directly into competitive success. They also translate into success later in life.

The "Better" Debater

- Is a gracious winner and a respectful loser.
- Gives strong rhetorical reasons for the probative force of their arguments.
- Makes the needs of and benefits to others the focus of the debate through her arguments, instead of focusing on her own competitive triumph.
- Argues through excellent evidence, but always makes her argument the focus, not her evidence. Better debaters are far more than their evidence.
- Debates dynamically, with enthusiasm and commitment, not passively.
- Sees the big picture, is aware of how ideas influence one another, and uses those relationships to enhance analysis in the debate.

- Knows the value of having a working command of the knowledge base. There is no substitute for knowing what it is you are debating about.
- Understands the need for organization in order to identify the critical tipping points in the debate.
- Portrays an image of an intelligent person who is seeking to understand and discover the truth.

THEY WIN WHEN THEY ARE SUPPOSED TO WIN.

The "Not Better" Debater

- Becomes frustrated when debate success isn't easy or automatic. Loses the benefits of debating through lack of determination.
- Whines that everything is against her—judges, situations, other teams, and fate.
- Fails to show respect to all participants—opponents, judges, and tournament hosts.
- Speaks from a position of privilege. She demands that you trust and accept her ideas over those of others without demonstrating them.
- Fails to make connections between various issues and arguments in the debate.
- Speaks only in generalities or only in specifics, not understanding that both the big picture and the line by line are important at all times.
- Fails to have fun in the debate. Her attitude causes others not to enjoy the experience.
- Fails to pay rigorous attention to the judge's critique, and thus learns from neither her failures nor her successes.
- Fails to focus during the debate at hand, allowing her mind to wander and outside events to distract her.

THEY LOSE WHEN THEY COULD WIN.

20

How the Decision
Gets Made

Each judge is unique, but most use several common methods to weigh the issues in the debate and determine the winner. These methods almost always focus on the arguments being made as opposed to issues of style and delivery. Policy debating is more about the issues than oratorical skills. Certainly good delivery is important because it more effectively showcases the issues being debated, but in making decisions judges almost always focus on the issues. As the name of this debate format suggests, each team supports a policy that it defines in the early stages of the debate, and then it argues over the merits and demerits of the competing policies. The judge is usually asking the question "Which policy (affirmative or negative) is better?"

If topicality is not an issue, the judge balances the arguments of one team against those of another. The issue of topicality precedes the consideration of all of the other issues in the debate because it claims that the affirmative team has proposed a policy outside of the topic stipulated for the debate, and thus should lose on that issue alone. However, if that issue is not present or once it is resolved in favor of the affirmative, then the other issues in the debate are awarded to one of the two sides in the debate and weighed against one another.

The judge, at the conclusion of the debate, looks at her flowsheet and decides who has won the various issues in the debate and with what probative force each of these issues should be given in the decision. Then, she uses a weighing process to determine which of the two policies has been established to be superior in the debate. Below are two graphic representations that will help you understand the process.

Tuna's Equation

While not an accomplished mathematician by any means, I have found it useful to express the weighing process in a mathematical form because some people can better understand it that way and many judges make their decisions in this fashion. This equation basically states that if the advantages of the affirmative policy system outweigh the advantages of the negative policy system, then the affirmative wins the debate. If the advantages of the negative policy system outweigh the affirmative advantages, then the negative wins the debate.

Here are the elements in this equation. The order in which they are presented emphasizes the order in which they are presented in the debate.

S = Affirmative significance established
The harm the affirmative claims exists in the present system or the potential advantage that is not being achieved

I = Degree to which status quo cannot solve
The affirmative's claim of why and how the present system fails to solve this problem or gain this potential advantage

V = Affirmative solvency established
The proven extent to which the affirmative plan can solve the problem the affirmative has outlined or the degree to which the affirmative plan achieves the potential advantage

D = Risk of disadvantage unique to affirmative

The demonstrated disadvantage that the negative proves will take place if the affirmative plan is adopted, and to what extent it would not happen in the absence of the affirmative plan

CCP = Competitive counterplan advantage
The negative's evaluation of the counterplan as an alternative to the affirmative plan. It is only relevant to the debate if the negative shows it as a reasonable alternative to the plan, and thus competitive with the plan.

Here's how a judge would use the equation to decide the debate:

$[S(I)V] > D = AFF$
If the harm that cannot be solved by the present system and is solved by the plan is greater than the disadvantage to the plan, the judge would vote affirmative.

$[S(I)V] < D = NEG$
If the harm that cannot be solved by the present system and is solved by the plan is less than the disadvantage to the plan, the judge would vote negative.

$[S(I)V] > D + CCP = AFF$
If the harm that cannot be solved by the present system and is solved by the plan is greater than the disadvantage to the plan and the advantage of the competitive counterplan, the judge would vote affirmative.

$[S(I)V] < D + CCP = NEG$
If the harm that cannot be solved by the present system and is solved by the plan is less than the disadvantage to the plan and the advantage of the competitive counterplan, the judge would vote negative.

If S = 10,000 lives, I = .8, V = .5, and D = 5,000 lives, who wins?

Why, the negative, of course. Let me give an example.

Imagine that the topic is that the U.S. federal government should require engineering changes in automobiles to increase safety.

If the affirmative proves that 10,000 people die each year from rear end collisions, that 80% of these deaths are not prevented by existing mechanisms such as safety training and following distance regulations, that their plan of placing blinking special bright lights in the rear of each car would prevent 50% of these deaths, but the negative shows that these mechanisms will cause people to drive more recklessly (a theory called safety compensation, where we tend to use devices that we feel are made "safer" in a more reckless fashion), causing an increase in accidents leading to 5,000 additional fatalities, then the negative will have won the debate.

The affirmative has 10,000 lives × .8 × .5 = 4,000 lives, which is less than the disadvantage of 5,000 lives.

Note that elements S, D, and CCP establish quantities and that elements I and V indicate a percentage that modifies these quantities. Of course, things are rarely this clear in the debate, but nevertheless the judge quite often awards the various issues and then feeds them into this sort of decision formula. By being aware of this equation and how it operates, you can argue in ways that can influence the decision in your favor.

Aunt Bluebell's Scales

A second weighing process views the affirmative and the negative as different sides of an imaginary scale; when the scales tip to one side, that side has won the debate. This imagery has been borrowed from an advertising campaign in which the fictional character "Aunt Bluebell" urges you to buy paper towels that were "heavier," and therefore better. She held up two different paper towels and said, "Weigh it for yourself, honey." This is what the judge would be doing.

This weighing process is a scale, and each team tries to add things to its side of the scale as well as remove things from the other team's side of the scale. The scale must tip in your direction at the end of the debate.

Certain elements stack directly on one side of the scale or the other, while other elements influence whether those elements reach the scale or not. As a strategic debater you are looking for the "tipping point" issue that can make the scale tip toward your side. This diagram should assist you in understanding how to locate such issues.

"Weigh it for yourself, honey!"

◯ = policy position advocated (plan)	A+	= added to affirmative
▢ = impact established	A-	= subtracted from affirmative
◯ = arguments modifying impacts	N+	= added to negative
	N-	= subtracted from negative

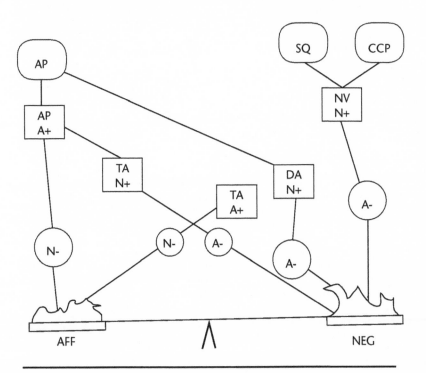

You can learn some important lessons from this simple model of the weighing process:

- To win, you need to establish real impacts and benefits of your policy.
- It is difficult to win the debate by just trying to move items from the other team's side of the scales.
- It is important to establish the quantities of your policy as well as stop the other team from piling too much on its side.

Remember that these two methods are simplifications of how judges go about weighing issues and deciding the winner. They do, however, explain some of the dynamics at work and can therefore enable you to better influence that decision.

21

Cross-Application of Ideas

One of the most difficult concepts for debaters to understand is how various issues relate to one another. We saw earlier how the issues interact to influence the decision. For example, there may be a huge harm in the present system, but it means little unless the affirmative can show that its plan will substantially reduce that harm.

Here is a simple chart that more experienced debaters have found useful for understanding interrelationships. It is also a clue to how debaters can find, inside of each type of issue, ways to relate that issue to others in the debate.

This is a puzzle. It explains how different issues in a debate can affect each other. Along the top of the chart we see the various issues that might exist in a debate. Along the side we see how each issue can relate to the others.

This diagram will help you understand how different issues interact in the debate. Let's look at the issues from left to right. The negative team may offer a topicality argument contending that the plan (or some portion of it) offered by the affirmative is not within the topic and therefore is invalid. This can relate to other issues:

Topicality: it might contradict the definition or interpretation suggested in other topicality arguments.

How Issues Relate to Each Other

TYPE OF ARGUMENT	Topicality	Significance Inherency	Solvency Aff	Solvency Neg	Disadvantage
Topicality	Contradict on definition, interpretation	—	No solvency from untopical mech	same	Part of plan which is untopical may be needed to get the disadvantage
	Significance Contradict	Aff gets no credit for what SQ can solve	Only gets credit for what they solve	Determines amount of significance plan can't solve for	Weight against it
	Inherency	Contradict	Plan fails to overcome inherent barriers	Other inherencies circumvention	Backlash arguments
		Solvency Aff	Contradictions	indicts solvency of plan	Disad may depend on solvency
			Solvency Neg	Contradict	Conceding solvency may take out a disadvantage
				Disadvantage	Contradictions: 3 tests

Solvency: the affirmative cannot claim to solve a problem with a non-topical portion of the plan, and would therefore get no credit for doing so.

Disadvantage: the negative cannot claim that a portion of the plan would cause a disadvantage *if* that portion is shown to be non-topical. While this could be done on an "even if" basis ("Even if this portion of the plan is topical, it will still lead to a disadvantage"), the relationship between these issues is still important to remember.

If we look at the right-hand side of the page and trace the argument relationships from top to bottom, we can further see these relationships. A negative team might offer a disadvantage to the adoption of the affirmative plan (the plan will cause something bad to happen) and this can be related to many other types of issues in the debate:

Significance: the disadvantage weighs against the reason why the affirmative states the plan should be adopted. If the plan causes a problem larger than the problem identified by the affirmative, then the negative would surely win the debate.

Inherency: often, in identifying barriers that prevent the status quo from solving the problem, the affirmative shows various attitudes against the plan that might exist in the population. These affirmative arguments can be used to build "backlash" arguments that indicate that the plan would not be properly implemented because so many people oppose it, or they might be used to compose a disadvantage that angry citizens will do something harmful or counterproductive if the plan is forced on them.

Solvency: (both affirmative and negative arguments): there are times when a negative disadvantage assumes that the affirmative actually solves the problem. For example, the affirmative may argue that the plan saves a considerable amount of resources, and the negative might argue that those resources will be utilized after the plan's adoption in a harmful way, such as funding military spending or dangerous forms of biological research. However, if the negative is going to offer such an argument, it must not argue that the plan will not save resources, as that eliminates the link to the disadvantage from the affirmative plan. If the negative is going to argue that gaining an advantage would be bad, it must avoid claiming that the plan will not succeed in gaining the advantage.

Disadvantage: when the negative offers more than one disadvantage to the adoption of the affirmative plan, they must not contradict each other. For example, one disadvantage that claims that "the free market is good because government intervention is bad for business" should not, in the next disadvantage, claim that "government intervention is needed to protect the public from profiteers." Very often negative teams do not fully understand these relationships. To find a contradiction, use three tests:

1. Do the causal or link claims of the two disadvantages contradict each other?
2. Do the two disadvantages make different assumptions about the world?
3. Do the two disadvantages claim contradictory harms?

One useful exercise is to take a recent debate and use the chart above to trace the ways in which the issues related to each other, and think about how you could have taken advantage of these relationships.

22

Evolving Arguments: Strategic Handling of Disadvantages

Arguments in the debate can evolve in very sophisticated ways. To win, you must be aware of the change and how it may influence the decision. One example of this evolution is how a disadvantage can develop. The explanation is rather complex for a new debater, but experienced debaters will find the lesson very useful.

Disadvantages can have an infinite number of fates, which you, as an affirmative or a negative team, can control. Sometimes the negative team would like a disadvantage that the affirmative has answered well to just go away so that the negative team can focus on other issues. Sometimes the negative would like to narrow the debate to just one disadvantage. Sometimes the affirmative may "link-turn" ("We solve this disadvantage with our plan") or "impact-turn" ("This result of this disadvantage is good, not bad") a disadvantage, and the negative will need to neutralize this offensive move. Here are six of the most common fates in policy debates:

1. Kick out of a disadvantage when there are no turns
2. Kick out of a disadvantage when there turns
3. Extend the disadvantage if there is nothing but turns
4. Lose the disadvantage by dropping affirmative answers
5. Deal with an affirmative double turn
6. Win a disadvantage by being complete in extending the arguments

Please consult the sample flowsheet as you go along, and it will help to graphically represent the points being made.

1. *Kick out of a disadvantage when there are no turns*
Let us assume that the affirmative plan will massively increase funding for the construction of alternative energy facilities such as solar cell farms and wind turbines. A lot of up-front capital spending will be needed before any benefit is accrued. The negative argues that there is a limited amount of capital in the credit markets and that the plan will pull available capital toward these alternative energy projects and away from the housing sector. Interest rates will rise; home foreclosures will escalate and the economy will be damaged; and needed housing stock will not be built. Sometimes the affirmative has great answers to your disadvantage that you would like to dismiss so that you can spend your time more productively on other issues. Here are some steps for doing so in a negative speech.

1. Concede specific responses given in the 2AC (such as 1. No link), indicating you agree with what the affirmative has said. For example, the affirmative might claim that this disadvantage "will not happen because it will be financed by tax increases, not through the capital market," and you can agree with it.
2. Explain how this concession makes the disadvantage irrelevant because the plan does not cause it.
3. Note that "no" answers are called turns so that the affirmative does not try to claim later that they have "turned" this disadvantage, making it a new reason to vote for them.
4. Explain that new turns or reinterpretations are not allowed in rebuttals.
5. Note that this disadvantage is now irrelevant to the debate.

2. *Kick out of a disadvantage when there are turns*
• The negative team would like this argument to go away, but since the affirmative has offered arguments that function as "turns," you can-

not just ignore or concede them. You must kick out of them, not just drop them. Otherwise, the turns create a new reason to vote affirmative. You can most often kick out of such a disadvantage by conceding specific affirmative answers and using them to eliminate the other answers the affirmative has that are turns. Once again, we will use the example of an affirmative case that funds a huge expansion of alternative energy resources. The disadvantage has argued that this will make it difficult for banks to loan money, because the cost of the plan will increase interest rates. When money is used by the plan, it reduces the supply of available money in the economy and thus makes loaning money more expensive, since whatever is in short supply costs more. This would disrupt a delicate banking system that is necessary for a stable and healthy economy.

- Identify contradictions: Answers from the 2AC 2 and 3 contradict, so they cancel each other out. One says the disadvantage will not happen and the other says the disadvantage will happen no matter what. Tell the judge that a confused negative team should not be rewarded.
- Concede answers to eliminate the link turn: This is how you would concede specific answers to take out the link turn. Conceding answers to take out the link turn (affirmative stops or solves problem disadvantage is about):
  1. No link. If plan does not cause it, does that eliminate the link turn?
     - NO: There may be other causes, especially if it is linear disadvantage. In fact, if argument 3 is valid and it is going to happen anyway, it is important to adopt the plan to solve the problem with banks.
  2. Won't happen. The argument is that the banks are very strong and they are not threatened by additional spending, even huge amounts. If internal link is gone, does that eliminate the link turn?
     - YES: If it isn't going to happen, they don't get credit for solving it.

3. Not unique. The argument is that banks are already in trouble and will collapse anyway. If it is going to happen anyway, does that eliminate the link turn?
   - NO: In fact, it makes the turn better. It is going to happen, so we better have the plan so we can solve it [most common error].
4. No significance. This argues that the banks may be hurt, but this will not spread to the entire economy. The Federal Deposit Insurance Corporation will make sure that people do not lose their money even if the banks are in trouble. If it is not bad, does that eliminate the link turn?
   - YES: The negative can turn it, but there is no impact. Caution: there may be SOME impact, in which case the answer is NO.
- Concede answers to take out the impact turn. Now, let us take the same disadvantage example but assume that all of the turns are "impact turns" (where the claim is that these are not bad results, but good results) and not link turns. Just suppose that the 2AC answers 5, 6, 7, 8, and 9 are impact turns, saying that the effect of this disadvantage would be good, not bad. The argument is that the current banking system is an outdated concept, and that if the banks were severely damaged, we would convert to new and better ways of handling and investing funds. Conceding specific answers can take out the impact turn (affirmative says the disadvantage result is good, not bad):
1. No link. The plan will not hurt the banks is the affirmative answer. If the plan does not lead to the disadvantage and does not hurt the banks, does that take out the impact turn?
   - YES: If X is good, but there is ZERO X caused, no impact.
2. Won't happen. The argument is that the banks are very strong and they are not threatened by additional spending, even huge amounts. If the internal link is gone, does that take out the impact turn?
   - YES: If it won't happen, it makes no difference if it is good or bad.

3. Not unique. The argument is that banks are already in trouble and will collapse anyway. If it is going to happen anyway, does that take out the impact turn?
   - YES: It happens if you vote affirmative or negative, so whether it is good or bad is irrelevant.
4. No significance. The Federal Deposit Insurance Corporation will make sure that people do not lose their money even if the banks are in trouble. If it is not bad, does that eliminate the impact turn?
   - NO: If it is not bad, it can still be good (impact turn claim). Plus, the harm taken out is the harm to consumers, not the harm to the banks themselves.

3. *Extend the disadvantage if there is nothing but turns*

For this concept we will use the example of the affirmative claiming to provide a guaranteed annual income to every citizen because that will reduce poverty. The disadvantage on the sample flowsheet argues that this will massively increase the demand for goods and services, leading to a rapid expansion of the economy. The rapid expansion of the economy, according to the negative, would be bad because rapid economic growth causes environmental damage and increased income disparities between the rich and the poor. The affirmative has responded with eight link turns, arguing that economic growth is not bad, but very, very good. This is a bad situation for the negative. The negative cannot eliminate the turns by conceding other answers, because there are none. Here are some techniques to keep in mind.

- Look for repeats. 1 and 7 (decrease war and increase peace), 4 and 8 (decrease pollution, protect the environment). These are not independent turns but just the same thing restated.
- Look for shared assumptions and defeat those assumptions. For example, the affirmative's turn arguments assume that the growth takes place all across the population, whereas it triggers a rise in spending and living standards mostly among those in poverty now.

- Evaluate how much of each turn the affirmative gets given the original link. For example, the affirmative plan causes $1B growth, which the negative says is bad. Affirmative says, no, since growth is good because it stops war. Affirmative does not get credit for stopping war, just credit for solving as much war as $1B growth will solve.
- Offer a new affirmative scenario in 2AC to outweigh. The 2AC can claim that the guaranteed annual income will stop a coming social conflict between the rich and the poor in America, and that this will disrupt the entire chain of reasoning used by the negative.
- Show turns are of no value; "No war is coming" would be a response to 1 and 7.
- Original disadvantage outweighs turns (growth is more bad than good). (Affirmative causes more growth than the extent of poverty it solves.)
- Answer the turns one by one, disproving each one. Once the turns are disposed of, the original disadvantage stands alone and undenied.

4. *Lose the disadvantage by dropping affirmative answers*

Here the negative deals with all affirmative answers except one, in this case the #4 answer. Affirmative then focuses all its attention on that one answer, really building it up. Affirmative saves time and negative fails to win disadvantage.

5. *Deal with an affirmative double turn*

The double turn is a heinous debate mistake made by the affirmative in the example on the flowsheet in disadvantage number five. The affirmative basically creates a new argument against itself when it both turns the link and the impact. In this example, you have argued that the plan does not cause X; in fact it stops all of X (link turn). You also argued that impact Y is not bad, it is actually good (impact turn). You are saying: "We give you less of a good thing." In the example on the flowsheet, the affirmative has said 1. The plan solves for inflation, but it has also said 5. Inflation is actually a good thing to have happen. This would be an independent reason to vote against the affirmative (especially if impact is large).

How should you handle this on either side?

Negative: When the affirmative double turns itself, connect the two, show it is a new disadvantage and explain it, impact it, say that it gets no new answers, and then show how other affirmative answers are irrelevant.

Affirmative: Explain how the two turns are of the same type, so it is not a double turn. Show how your other responses would take out one of the turns (see #2 above about conceding answers to take out the link or impact turn), so there is no double turn. For example, if answer #2 is accepted and the entire disadvantage will not happen, the double turn is irrelevant. If answer #3 is true and it "will not happen," the double turn is irrelevant. If #4 is true and the inflation phenomenon is empirically false, then the double turn would be irrelevant. These answers indicate that the entire inflation will not take place, so there is nothing to double turn. The link turn is eliminated because there will be no inflation to solve, and the impact turn is eliminated because there is no inflation to produce good effects.

6. Win a disadvantage by being complete in extending the arguments
You win a disadvantage on the negative by defeating all of the affirmative answers. The example on the flowsheet shows how this is done.

- Be complete. Answer all of the opposition's answers.
- Gang up—do more than the opposition does.
- Always indicate impact of disadvantage.
- Have a story for all the components: link, internal link, brink (if threshold), linearity (if linear), impact size, probability of impact, uniqueness (if threshold).

Picture of Six Disadvantages

Capital X indicates that a piece of evidence is introduced to support this point.

1NC	2AC
1. Plan causes harm to housing sector A. Link B. Internal link C. Impact	1. No link. 2. Not true. X 3. No internal link. 4. Impact is very small. X 5. Data used is flawed. X
2. Plan causes harm to banking sector A. Link B. Internal link C. Impact	1. No link. Plan would not cause. X 2. Will not happen. X 3. Not unique, will happen anyway. X 4. Impact is very small. X 5. Link turn. Plan would solve. X 6. Link turn. Plan would solve. X 7. Link turn. Plan would solve. X 8. Link turn. Plan would solve. X 9. Link turn. Plan would solve. X
3. Plan causes harmful economic growth A. Link B. Internal link C. Impact	1. Turn: economic growth decreases war. X 2. Turn: economic growth decreases poverty. X 3. Turn: economic growth decreases racism. X 4. Turn: economic growth decreases pollution. X 5. Turn: economic growth increases democracy. X 6. Turn: economic growth increases personal happiness. X 7. Turn: economic growth increases peace. X 8. Turn: economic growth protects the environment. X
4. Plan causes war A. Link B. Internal link C. Impact	1. Answer. X 2. Answer. X 3. Answer. X 4. Answer. X 5. Answer. X 6. Answer. X
5. Plan causes harmful inflation A. Link B. Internal link C. Impact	1. Link turn. Our plan stops this. X 2. Not true. X 3. Will not happen. X 4. Empirically false. X 5. Impact turn. It would be good. X
6. Plan causes extermination of indigenous people A. Link B. Internal link C. Impact	1. Answer. X 2. Answer. X 3. Answer. X 4. Answer. X

2NC/1NR	1AR	2NR

1. Defeat the answer.
2. Defeat the answer.
3. Defeat the answer.
4. NOTHING SAID
5. Defeat the answer
6. Defeat the answer

Negative drops answer #4; it is a great argument; the evidence is excellent. Here is more evidence showing that this dropped answer defeats the disadvantage. X X

---

1. Defeat the answer.	1. Defend the answer.	1. Defeat answer again. X
2. Defeat the answer. X	2. Defend the answer.	2. Defeat answer again.
3. Defeat the answer.	3. Defend the answer.	3. Defeat answer again. X
4. Defeat the answer. X	4. Defend the answer.	4. Defeat answer again.

Read more impact evidence. X X

Extend the impact, talk about how it outweighs the case.

Appendix 1: Videos and Web Sites

Videos

In cooperation with the World Debate Institute and the Lawrence Debate Union at the University of Vermont, I have produced a series of videos for instructional use.

You will need to have the latest versions of the following software:

iTunes

http://www.apple.com/itunes/download/

Those videos saved as podcasts (.m4v suffix) are best viewed with iTunes.

QuickTime

http://www.apple.com/quicktime/download/

Make sure to get the one suited for your computer.

RealPlayer

http://www.real.com/player

Get the free version; you may have to look for it a bit.

VIDEOS FOR POLICY DEBATERS

Some of these links may download a small file to your computer, especially if it has the suffix for RealPlayer (.rm). If the video does not start right away, click on this file and it should start.

SAMPLE POLICY DEBATE (FREE)

Here is a sample policy debate on school uniforms with shortened speech times designed for a new debater.

Part One

http://video.google.com/videoplay?docid=4403190344471700804

Part Two
http://video.google.com/videoplay?docid=-7466510569865712849

POLICY DEBATE INSTRUCTION VIDEOS (FREE)

A huge list of policy debate videos can be found at
http://debate.uvm.edu/policyvideo.html

A comprehensive set of online instructional videos for novice debaters
can be found at
http://debate.uvm.edu/watchnovicepolicyvideo.html

A comprehensive set of online instructional videos for intermediate policy debaters can be found at
http://debate.uvm.edu/watchintermpolicyvideo.html

A comprehensive set of online instructional videos for advanced policy
debaters can be found at
http://debate.uvm.edu/watchadvpolicyvideo.html

TRAINING RESOURCES (FOR PURCHASE)

Comprehensive sets of debate training materials in CD and DVD formats
can be found at
http://debate.uvm.edu/ee.html

CLASSROOM LECTURE SERIES: CRITICAL ADVOCACY (FREE)

An educational series for students, teachers, and citizens interested in
critical communication skills. The emergence of a global community
of ideas and discourse requires successful individuals to develop critical
advocacy skills—to develop strong ideas, to present them effectively, to
defend them skillfully, and to critically analyze opposing ideas. Based on
decades of international experience, this series will provide you with the
ideas and training you need to succeed.
http://debate.uvm.edu/critadv.html

Web Sites for Policy Debate

Listed in order of value to policy debaters

Debate Central
http://debate.uvm.edu
The world's largest debate instruction Web site. Has comprehensive materials for policy debate and many other formats.

International Debate Education Association
http://idebate.org
While not emphasizing policy debate, this Web site can tell you about debate in other countries and also offers clues for coming up with arguments in the DEBATABASE section.

World Debate Institute
http://debate.uvm.edu/wdiblog/wdiblog/Blog/Blog.html
This is a summer program that offers training in policy debate and other formats for high school students, college students, and teachers.

National Forensic League
http://www.nflonline.org/Main/HomePage
This is the Web site of the organizing body for high school speech and debate in the United States. One of main events is a policy debate. You might want to look at the rules and guidelines for policy debate found in the district and national manuals.

Cross Examination Debate Association
http://cedadebate.org
This is one of the two organizing groups for policy debate at the college level. Here you can find the current policy debate topic for college debaters.

National Debate Tournament
http://groups.wfu.edu/NDT/
This is the other group that organizes college policy debate and holds an exclusive tournament at the end of the year that teams must qualify for in order to attend.

Global Debate Blog

http://globaldebateblog.blogspot.com

This Web site contains news and events from all around the world of debating. Here you can find out what other parts of the world are debating and how.

Debate Videoblog

http://debatevideoblog.blogspot.com

This Web site offers many different types of instructional videos and sample debates in many different formats, including policy debate.

Associated Leaders of Urban Debate

http://www.debateleaders.org

This group assists urban schools in starting and developing debate programs. Its focus is largely on policy debate.

National Association for Urban Debate Leagues

http://www.naudl.org

This group also assists urban schools in debating.

Debate Video Archive

http://www.uvm.edu/~debate/watch/

This is an archive with links to many debate-related videos. They are not annotated or described, but there are hundreds and they are all free.

Appendix 2: Sample Flowsheet

1AC	1NC	2AC	2NC 1NR	1AR	2NR	2AR
Contention one: Harms A. Sub	1. Argument Reason Evidence	Answer Reason Evidence				
Reason Evidence Reason Evidence	2. Argument Logical Challenge	1. Answer Logical Point	Rebuttal Logical Point	?	This is a big deal Explains why	No it isn't Final Answer
	3. Argument Reason Evidence	2. Answer Reason Evidence Answer Reason Evidence	Rebuttal Reason Evidence Reason Evidence	Rebuttal Logical Point		
B. Sub Reason Evidence Reason Evidence	1. Argument Logical Challenge	Answer Logical Point	Rebuttal Logical Point	Rebuttal Logical Point		
	2. Argument Reason Evidence	Answer Reason Evidence				
	3. Argument Reason Evidence	1. Answer Logical Point 2. Answer Reason Evidence				
	4. Argument Logical Challenge	1. Answer Logical Point	Rebuttal Logical Point	Rebuttal Logical Point	Rebuttal Logical Point	Final Answer
		2. Answer Logical Point	Rebuttal Reason Evidence	?	This is a big deal	No it isn't Explains why

Appendix 3: Sample Brief

Democracy Is Not So Good [Frontline]

(__) DEMOCRACY DOESN'T PROTECT ALL [TAGLINE]
Noberto Bobbio, Political Theorist, WHICH SOCIALISM? MARXISM, SOCIALISM, AND DEMOCRACY, 1987, p. 43. [CITATION]

The objection raised to bourgeois democracy is that it has conceded freedom to the citizen and not to the producer, the worker. But there will be no new or renewed democracy; in fact there will be no democracy at all, if the freedom of the producer is not accompanied and underpinned by the freedom of the citizen. [BODY OF EVIDENCE QUOTATION]

(__) NO DIFFERENCE IN WAR BETWEEN DEMOCRACIES AND NON-DEMOCRACIES
Erich Weede, Prof. Political Science, Univ. Cologne, Journal of Conflict Resolution, 1984, p. 649.
Whether a nation enjoys democratic rule or suffers from dictatorship, the risk of getting involved in war is the same. This has been one of the findings of Weede. Nor was this an isolated finding.

(__) TRADITIONAL DEMOCRATIC THEORY FAILS
Carol C. Gould, Prof. Philosophy, Stevens Inst. of Tech., RETHINKING DEMOC-RACY, 1990, p. 3.

The premise of this book is that there is a need for a new theory of democracy and for a rethinking of its philosophical foundations. This need derives, in the first instance, from the inadequacies of the traditional democratic theory of liberal in-dividualism, which, despite the strength of its emphasis on individual liberty, fails to take sufficiently into account the requirements of social cooperation and social equality.

( ) DEMOCRACY FAILS ON THE INTERNATIONAL STAGE
Carol C. Gould, Prof. Philosophy, Stevens Inst. of Tech., RETHINKING DEMOC-RACY, 1990, p. 307.

Democratic theory with its joint requirements of self-determination, on the one hand, and human rights and justice, on the other, seems to break down when extended to the domain of international relations. For here, the principle of self-determination as the self-determination of nations would appear to require the recognition of state sovereignty and thus the principle of nonintervention in the internal affairs of any state by another. By contrast, the principles of human rights and of justice would seem to require intervention in the affairs of other states when such rights are violated, and such intervention would seem to violate the right of self-determination of nations and the sovereignty of states.

Glossary

Add-on advantage
A new advantage presented by the affirmative in 2AC.

Affirmative
The team that supports the resolution.

Affirmative case
The part of the affirmative position that demonstrates that there is a need for change because there is a serious problem (need) that the present system cannot solve (inherency) but which is nonetheless, solvable (solvency).

Affirmative plan
The policy action advocated by the affirmative. Usually indicates an agent to take the action, the specification of that action, financing details, and other elements selected by the affirmative team.

Agent counterplans
A counterplan that argues that the plan you are implementing through one agent of change, should instead be implemented by another agent of change.

Agent of the resolution (or Agent of change)
That power called for by the resolution to carry out resolutional action.

A priori
Literally, prior to. Usually an argument that indicates that a particular issue should be resolved before all others. Frequently used to argue that procedural concerns such as topicality should be considered before substantive issues such as advantages.

Attitudinal inherency
This type of inherency identifies an unwillingness of those in power in the present system to take corrective measures to solve the harm cited by the affirmative.

Audience
Those who are physically present during the debate.

Best definition standard for topicality
Usually argued as a topicality standard by the negative team. The negative argues that the judge must choose the best definition offered in the round in order to decide whether the plan is topical. Affirmatives often argue that there is no need to choose, since a definition only needs to be reasonable (not "best") for debate purposes. "Best" is determined by arguments made by the negative, such as source, context, date, specificity, etc.

Blow up
Negative will take one argument or issue from 1NC and expand on it for many, many minutes in 2NC.

Brief
A prepared page with evidence and arguments already structured.

Brink
The point at which a disadvantage actually begins to happen. This concept explains why a disadvantage impact will happen if the plan is passed but is not happening now, because we are "at the brink" but not "over the brink" of this event actually taking place.

Burden of proof
The responsibility a debater has of proving an argument he offers in a complete fashion.

Burden of rebuttal
The burden of refuting issues offered by opponents.

Card
A piece of evidence used to prove an argument. In the "old days" evidence was put on index cards and used in the debate.

Case
The complete argument for the resolution offered in the 1AC.

Categorical deduction
An argument stating that all members of a category have certain characteristics, placing something or someone within that category, and thus claiming that it must have those characteristics.

Circumvention
A negative argument proving that the plan will not solve the problem. People are opposed to the plan (motivation), they will find a way to "get around" the plan (mechanism), and this will stop the plan from being effective (impact).

Citation
Where a piece of evidence (or "card") came from. Usually includes author, title, date, and page number. A citation must be sufficient to allow someone to locate that evidence again.

Clash
Actively attacking and refuting positions of the opposing team.

Comparative advantage case
A type of affirmative case that argues that the status quo isn't necessarily harmful but that things would be better with the plan.

Competition
A burden of the negative counterplan. The counterplan competes if it is a reasonable substitute for the affirmative, so in voting for the counterplan, the judge would be rejecting the affirmative plan. A counterplan is competitive if it would be better to adopt just the counterplan rather than the affirmative plan and the counterplan.

Conditional
Debaters stipulate that their argument is "conditional" in that they can discard or drop that argument or issue whenever they wish or when certain conditions are met.

Conditional counterplan
A plan tentatively presented by a negative team but one that can be dropped if undesirable without forfeiture of the debate.

Constructive speeches
The first four speeches of the debate, where teams build and elaborate on their issues and advocacy.

Contention
A major point in the debate. Affirmative cases are often built of such contentions.

Context
1. The relationship of the evidence read in the debate to the original source material. Evidence must be consistent with the meaning of the evidence as it is written in the original source.
2. A standard for evaluating topicality arguments that is used to determine if the definition offered in the debate is consistent with the meaning of the term in relationship to authors who write about the subject matter of the topic, or to determine if the definition offered in the debate is consistent with the meaning of the term in relationship to other terms in the resolution.

Contradiction
Two arguments are incompatible with each other, or there is a perceived conceptual tension between two ideas.

Co-option
The influence of outside parties hampering an agency's efforts to carry out its instructions.

Counterplan
The negative's "better solution" than the affirmative plan. A counterplan is like a "little affirmative case" and should have a plan and solvency as well as be competitive with the affirmative plan.

Counterplan advantages
Benefits that result from the adoption of the counterplan.

Counterplan non-topicality
The condition of a counterplan of being outside the resolution lest it become further justification of the resolution. Since the obligation of the negative is to "negate" the topic being debated, the negative should not propose a topical counterplan.

Cover
Dealing with an issue in a speech, either by refuting or rebuilding it, you have "covered" it.

Credibility

A quality a speaker has that makes the audience want to believe him. Usually audiences find speakers credible if they communicate well, have knowledge of the topic, and seem to be of good character.

Criteria

A decision rule or conceptual tool to be used in deciding who wins the debate. The term literally means the standards by which an argument should be evaluated. For example, if money were your only criteria for choosing a job, you would look at that factor over others. Never ignore any argument called a criteria, or all of your other arguments may be made irrelevant.

Critique/Kritik

An argument that establishes that the fundamental assumptions embodied by the other team are false or reprehensible.

Cross-examination

One debater questions another debater about issues in the debate that is taking place.

Cut evidence

To copy a portion of a book, magazine, or hearing onto a note card or brief.

Debatability

A concept related to topicality and other theoretical arguments. One team will claim that the other team's interpretation of the topic or the debate setting is inferior because it makes the essential debate process more difficult. For example, a topicality definition that is very broad might make the topic itself "undebatable" because it would have no real limits.

Debate

An equitably structured communication event about some topic of interest with opposing advocates alternating before an opportunity is given for decision.

Decision rule

An idea that tells the judge how to weigh and compare issues. For example, you might say in a debate about health care, "The decision in this debate should be for the team with the policy that best provides for the health of each citizen." Thus, the judge would focus on "health" as the decision rule. Always be wary of teams proposing a decision rule, as it usually favors them in the debate.

Disadvantage

Argument that the plan proposed by the other team will cause bad things to happen which would not have happened otherwise.

Disco

A term used to describe a type of debate strategy where a team takes advantage of the interrelationship among arguments in the debate to concede large portions of the opponent's arguments. The hope is that such a strategy will dismiss large portions of arguments and allow the team to focus the debate on issues favorable to its side of the question.

Discursive impact
An argument that the language used within the debate is more important than the issues debated. Discursive impacts are usually claimed by critiques.

Dispositional
An argument, usually a counterplan, that can be discarded by conceding competitiveness.

Double turn
This takes place when in answering a disadvantage, a team argues a link turn (we solve that problem) AND an impact turn (that problem is actually a benefit). Thus, it is saying that it stops a good thing from happening.

Drop (out)
When you do not discuss an issue or argument in a speech, you are considered to have "dropped" that argument or issue. Dropped issues or arguments are considered to be won by the last speech to discuss them in some detail.

Effects topicality
The affirmative claims that the plan itself is not topical, but that it leads to a topical condition or result.

Emory switch
A negative strategy involving presentation of plan attacks in first negative constructive and need or advantage attacks in second negative constructive.

Enforcement plank
A part of the affirmative plan providing assurance that the plan's mandates will be carried out, usually through a directive that a particular agency will oversee and ensure compliance with those mandates.

Evidence
Authoritative quoted published material entered into the debate to support the arguments being made.

Extension
Continuing to advance and elaborate on an issue through several speeches of the debate.

Existential inherency
With this kind of inherency, if the affirmative can demonstrate a massive problem exists, then it has met the burden of inherency by showing that the present system is not solving it.

Extratopicality
Advantages are extratopical when they stem from portions of the plan that are not topical action.

Fiat
The assumption that in order to decide the desirability of an alternative future, we first have to imagine that it exists. Thus, teams are not required to show that their plans "will" be adopted but that they "should" be adopted.

Field context
A topicality definition that is derived from the writings of experts on the subject of the resolution.

Flip
See Turn

Flow
Notes debaters take during a debate using a specific format.

Flow judge
An experienced judge who takes extensive notes during the debate.

Flowsheet
Paper used to keep track of the arguments in a debate.

Frontlines
Prepared answers to arguments that are anticipated from the opposing team.

Funding plank
The part of the plan naming or listing those sources that will supply the money that the plan requires.

Games theory
A paradigm for debate that views the debate as an educational game requiring fair rules to insure each participant has an equal chance of winning the game.

Generic arguments
Arguments, usually negative, that are general and apply to a wide range of affirmative cases or plans.

Generic disadvantage
A disadvantage designed to link to almost any conceivable affirmative plan.

Goals case
A type of affirmative case that claims a particular goal is sought by the status quo and that argues that the plan better meets that goal.

Grammatical context
A topicality definition that is derived from the relationship of terms in a consistent grammatical form with other terms in the resolution.

Ground
The positions teams must defend as affirmative or negative. Each team needs to have some "ground" to defend in order for the debate to be a fair contest. Thus, interpretations of the topic that leave the negative no "ground" to defend should be rejected because they are unfair.

Hasty generalization
An argument asserting that a judge cannot conclude that a resolution is true based on a minor or small example.

Hypothesis testing
One of many paradigms used to explain the debate process. It means that the focus of the debate is on testing the resolution as if it were a scientific hypothesis.

Hypothetical counterplan
See conditional counterplan.

Impact
Explanation of why something is important, and thus how it influences the outcome of the debate. Usually impacts need to be proven, not just assumed.

Impact turn
An argument that establishes that the supposed impact or harm claimed is actually not a bad thing but a good thing.

Independent advantage
An advantage that can justify adoption of a plan even if the other advantages claimed may not be true.

Inherency
Basic component of an affirmative case. Explains why the problem identified persists and why it is not being solved.

Internal link
Conceptual linkages and relationships between ideas. Part of a causal chain debaters construct in their arguments that hold them together.

Intrinsic
A situation in which a disadvantage is a necessary result of the affirmative plan that cannot be prevented in another way.

Jurisdiction
The parameters, provided by the topic, within which actors in the debate operate.

Justification
A rarely used negative argument asserting that the affirmative must have a reason for each part of the resolution.

Kick out
This is a tactic used to eliminate an argument from the debate. This can only be done only by the debater who originally made the argument. Thus, the negative may "kick out" of a disadvantage by conceding some of the affirmative's answers to it.

Label
The short form of the argument presented as a way to identify and preview the argument. "Democracy dos not guarantee solution of all problems" might be an argument label. After the label is given, it will have to be more completely developed in order to be accepted.

Legislative intent
A provision in a plan that future judgment of the meaning of the plan will be based on its advocate's speeches.

Link
A causal or correlative relationship between two ideas.

Link turn
An argument that establishes that a given policy does not cause a problem or disadvantage identified by the other team but actually works to solve that problem.

Minor repair
A non-resolutional small change in existing programs to solve the problem presented by the negative. It should not require structural change and should be within the philosophy of the present system.

Mutual exclusivity
Method for determining competition of the counterplan. If the affirmative plan and the negative counterplan cannot exist at the same time, they are competitive with each other.

Need
The problem that the affirmative hopes to solve; the area of affirmative significance.

Negative block
The second negative constructive and the first negative rebuttal; the two negative speeches in the middle of the debate.

Net benefits
Method for determining competition of the counterplan. If it would be more beneficial to adopt just the counterplan than both it and the affirmative plan, they are competitive with each other based on the concept of net benefits.

Off case
Issues such as counterplans, topicality arguments, disadvantages, or critiques offered by the negative that do not directly refute the affirmative case but introduce new issues arguing for its rejection.

Permutation
A test the affirmative uses to examine the competitiveness of the counterplan, in which it speculates on how the two plans might be merged.

Philosophical competition
A standard of competition for counterplans that argues that since the two plans under consideration have different philosophical approaches, they are exclusive of one another.

Plan
Proposal for policy action presented by the affirmative. Usually includes agent, action, extent, funding, enforcement, etc.

Plan attack
Arguments directed at an affirmative policy itself (e.g., plan-meet-need, disadvantage, workability).

Plan mandates
The resolutional action specified in the affirmative plan.

Plan-meet-need
An argument claiming that a plan does not solve the need. Usually a subdivided and structured argument presented in 2nd negative constructive.

Plan-side
That part of the flow on which arguments are written about the plan.

Plan spike
A non-topical element included in a plan to avoid a disadvantage.

Policy making
A philosophy that debate rounds should be evaluated from the perspective of pseudo-legislators weighing the advantages and disadvantages of two conflicting policy systems.

Political capital
The amount of good will a politician can muster to get policies enacted. In debate this argument says passing the plan will consume so much political capital that those enacting the plan will have to sacrifice other important issues on their political agendas. The political capital expended passing the plan sacrifices the political capital necessary to get other policies passed.

Political disadvantages
Arguments that indicate that the political consequences of passing the plan will lead to impacts that will outweigh the case.

Political focus
The ability of political leaders to concentrate on particular issues. In debate, the argument says that passing the affirmative plan will require so much energy and time that policy makers will be unable to get other, more important issues passed.

Political popularity
The approval rating of a politician. In debate, the argument considers the public approval of the plan. If the plan is unpopular, policy makers will lose credibility, making it nearly impossible to pass other, more important plans. If the plan is popular, it may boost the credibility of policy makers, making it easier for them to get other, less desirable plans passed.

Posting
A list of debates that have been scheduled at a tournament. The "posting" includes room, affirmative team, negative team, and judge(s).

Preemption or preempt
An argument designed to respond to an anticipated argument.

Prep time
Time between speeches when debaters prepare.

Presumption
An assumption that we should stay with the system that we have now; it operates against change and untried policies.

Prima facie
Latin for "at first glance." The requirement that the initial presentation of major issues in the debate should be "logically complete." It does not demand that the presentation be perfect.

Read evidence
In a policy debate, the requirement that a debater actually read passages from that evidence into the debate.

Reasonability
A topicality standard that indicates that the affirmative need only to offer a definition that is not excessively broad and would appear legitimate at first glance.

Rebuttals
Shorter, later speeches in the debate when the issues built in the constructive speeches are argued over.

Redundancy
This standard for counterplan competition argues that if the counterplan can achieve the affirmative advantage, then the affirmative has not demonstrated that the advantage is an inherent result of the resolution.

Refutation
The act of answering or criticizing ideas and issues presented by the other team.

Reify
Using language that makes "false" or "illusory" concepts seem real and/or legitimate. For example, some critics might say that advocating aid for minorities actually makes racism more legitimate because it "reifies" the idea of race. These critics argue that, because there is no biological basis for race, targeting people of specific races for help supports (or "reifies") the false notion of race, thus legitimizing racism.

Resolution
The topic of a particular debate.

Retrench
To reinforce the present system. Usually occurring in discussions of critiques, the argument says that the effect of a policy is to reinforce the prevailing attitudes in the status quo. Thus, the problems that exist won't be solved and may worsen.

Reverse voting issue
Often used when one team argues that something is a "voting issue." The other team can explain that if it is a voting issue one way, it should also be a voting issue the other way.

Risk analysis
The theory and procedure of claiming that 100% certainty is not needed to act and that the level of certainty that does exist is sufficient basis for policy decisions.

Sandbag
Saving the best evidence for an argument until the rebuttals, or presenting the impact for an argument later.

Scenario
A specification of a particular series of events. Usually consist of who, what, when, where, how, and why.

Shift
Changing advocacy in the middle of the debate from one position to another.

Should-would
The concept that the affirmative does not have to show that its proposal would be adopted, but that it should be adopted.

Significance
An explanation of the serious problems that exist now. Usually a component of the affirmative case.

Solvency
An explanation of how the plan proposed by the affirmative solves the problem it has identified. Usually a component of the affirmative case.

Spread
Making many, many arguments in an attempt to prevent the other team from answering them all.

Squirrel case
An affirmative approach that isolates an obscure area of the topic to justify the resolution.

Standards
Explanation and methods of evaluation that clarify why one interpretation of a word or phrase is superior to another. Usually part of topicality arguments. Also known as reasons to prefer.

Status quo
The existing state of affairs.

Stock issues
Standard points of controversy in policy disputes: harm, inherency, solvency, plan, disadvantages.

Subpoints
Substructure of a larger argument, contention, or observation.

Take out
A defensive answer to an argument. It claims that the argument is not true and should be eliminated from the debate.

Threshold
See Brink.

Time frame
Explanation of when a predicted or caused event will take place.

Topicality
The notion that the affirmative plan/negative counterplan should/should not fall within the conceptual boundaries of the resolution.

Turn or turn around or flip
"Turns the tables" on opponents. Argues that the problem raised by opponents is unique to the policy system they defend, not to the policy system they oppose. Thus, the plan may not cause the problem—it may solve it (turn).

Uniqueness
Whether something is an essential cause of a situation or scenario. That component of a disadvantage that illustrates that the disadvantage impact that the negative claims results only from the adoption of the affirmative plan, that is, the disadvantage impact would not occur absent the affirmative plan.

Voting issue
An argument stipulating that this issue alone, and its fate, should determine the decision in the debate. Often claimed for topicality issues.

Whole resolution or (whole res)
A generic debate argument that says that the resolution must be debated in a holistic manner to determine its probable truth. Usually the negative must establish some form of standard to measure when it is possible to induce the truth of the resolution.